Aquinas

AQUINAS

by Anthony Kenny

General Editor, Keith Thomas
PAST MASTERS SERIES

Hill and Wang · New York
A division of Farrar, Straus and Giroux

Library of Congress Cataloging in Publication Data
Kenny, Anthony John Patrick. Aquinas.
(Past masters series) Bibliography: p. Includes index.
1. Thomas Aquinas, Saint, 1225?-1274—Philosophy.
I. Series.   B765.T54K42 1980   189′.4   79-27404
ISBN 0-8090-2724-0   ISBN 0-8090-1407-6 pbk.

Preface

This is a book about Thomas Aquinas as a philosopher: it is written for readers who may not necessarily share his theological interests and beliefs. Apart from his commentaries on Aristotle, Aquinas wrote little of an explicitly philosophical nature; but his theological works, and especially his masterpiece the *Summa Theologiae*, contain philosophical insights which entitle him to be considered as one of the world's great philosophers.

The book is divided into three chapters. The first is an account of St Thomas's life and works and an assessment of his significance for contemporary philosophy. The second is a sketch of the major concepts of Aquinas's metaphysical system: it includes a discussion of the doctrine of Being, which is one of the most famous, but also the most overrated, elements in his philosophy. The third chapter is devoted to Aquinas's philosophy of mind, which is less well known but far more rewarding to study. The book concludes with a bibliographical note.

I am indebted to Professor A. C. Lloyd and Dr Henry Hardy for comments on an earlier draft of the book, and to Mrs Mary Bugge for typing the manuscript.

Balliol
31 January 1979

Contents

List of abbreviations

The following abbreviations have been used in referring to works of Aquinas:

C *De Virtutibus in Communi*, Rome, 1953. English translation: *On the Virtues in General*, trans. J. P. Reid, Providence, R. I., 1951.
E *De Ente et Essentia*, ed. L. Baur, Munster, 1933. English translation: *Being and Essence*, trans. A. Maurer, Toronto, 1949.
G *Summa contra Gentiles*: see Bibliographical Note.
M *In XII Libros Metaphysicorum*, ed. R. M. Spiazzi, Turin, 1950. English translation: *Commentary on the Metaphysics of Aristotle*, Chicago, 1961.
H *In Libros Peri Hermeneias*, ed. R. M. Spiazzi, Turin, 1955. English translation in *Aristotle on Interpretation – Commentary by St Thomas and Cajetan*, J. Oesterle, Milwaukee, 1962.
P *Quaestiones Disputatae de Potentia Dei*, ed. R. M. Spiazzi, Turin, 1949. English translation: *On the Power of God*, trans. L. Shapcote and others, Westminster, Maryland, 1952.
Q *Quaestiones Quodlibetales*, ed. R. M. Spiazzi, Rome, 1949.
S *Summa Theologiae*: see Bibliographical Note.
V *Quaestiones Disputatae de Veritate*, ed. R. M. Spiazzi, Turin, 1949. English translation: *Truth*, trans. R. W. Mulligan and others, Chicago, 1952.

S is usually cited by part, question, article, and (if applicable) objection or reply; thus 'I–II 3 2 ad 2' means: the reply to the second objection in the second article of the third question of the First Part of the Second Part (see below, p. 20). G is cited by book and chapter.

The translations given in the text are in general my own, though I am indebted to existing translations.

Aquinas

1 Life

Near the beginning of the year 1225 Thomas Aquinas was born in the castle of Roccasecca near Naples, the seventh son of Count Landulf of the great feudal house of Aquino. It was just ten years since King John of England had signed the Great Charter at Runnymede, and since the Spaniard Dominic de Guzman had gone to Rome to found the Order of Friars Preachers which bears his name. The major part of Europe, including what is now Britain, France, Germany and Italy, belonged to a single Latin culture in which the most powerful institutions were the Holy Roman Empire and the Roman Catholic Church. Latin Europe was bounded in Spain by the Muslim culture of Grenada and in the Balkans by the Greek empire of Byzantium; in Asia it maintained a precarious colony in the Crusader kingdom of Jerusalem. The Emperor Frederick II ruled from Germany to Sicily, and astounded his contemporaries by the cosmopolitan breadth of his interests: his ambitions conflicted with those of a succession of Popes and made the Italy of the early thirteenth century a theatre of constant strife.

At the age of five Thomas was sent by his father to the great Benedictine abbey of Monte Cassino: a monastery which was also a frontier-fortress between Frederick's Kingdom of Naples and the Papal States. He was received as an oblate: not quite an infant monk, yet with a greater expectation of monastic commitment than a modern schoolboy at a Benedictine preparatory school. After nine years of elementary studies he had his education interrupted when troops occupied the abbey in the course of a quarrel between Pope and Emperor. After a brief period at home, he was sent to the University of Naples, founded by the Emperor some fourteen years earlier as a counterweight to the Papal University of Bologna. There he studied the seven liberal arts of grammar, logic, rhetoric, arithmetic, geometry, music and astronomy. In studying the 'arts' of logic and astronomy he began his education in philosophy: he read Aristotle's logical treatises with the commentaries of later scholars and he was introduced to Aristotle's scientific and cosmological works by a teacher named Peter of Ireland.

In 1244 Thomas became a Dominican friar. His kinsfolk, who had looked forward to his becoming a Benedictine monk and abbot, were enraged. To the secular twentieth-century eye there may not seem a great difference between monks and friars, bound alike to obedience, celibacy and devotion; but a thirteenth-century aristocrat distinguished sharply between monks, who followed a stable calling of ancient respectability on well-endowed estates, and friars, who were new-fangled itinerant evangelists mingling with the urban poor and living by begging. Thomas's father was now dead, but the rest of his family made their displeasure so clear that the Dominicans decided to send him to Paris for safety. On the journey thither, resting with his companions by a spring in Tuscany, Thomas was kidnapped by his elder brothers and carried off to a family castle at Monte San Giovanni. Neither his mother's tears nor his brothers' force were able to strip him of the white tunic and black cloak of the Dominicans. But he was kept under house arrest at Roccasecca for more than a year before being allowed to rejoin his brethren.

While imprisoned Thomas composed two brief treatises on formal logic: a handbook on the fallacies liable to occur in standard patterns of reasoning, dedicated to 'noblemen reading arts', and a fragment on modal propositions (sentences about necessity and possibility), composed probably for a former classmate at Naples. Better known than Thomas's first efforts at philosophical composition is the story of the trial of his resolve of chastity. Either out of pity or out of cunning, his brothers one night sent a seductive wench to his cell to offer herself for his pleasure. Thomas leapt up, seized a brand from the fire and drove her from the room. He fell into a sleep in which he dreamt that angels bound his loins in token of perpetual chastity. 'From that time onwards', says his earliest biographer, 'it was his custom always to avoid the sight and company of women – except in case of necessity or utility – as a man avoids snakes.'

Some time after his release from Roccasecca Thomas went to the Dominican house of studies at Cologne, where he studied from 1248 until 1252 under Albert the Great. Albert was some twenty-five years his senior, a founder member of the Dominicans in Germany and a man of keen scientific curiosity and prodigious indiscriminate learning. Under him, Thomas learnt to appreciate the encyclopaedic genius of Aristotle, whose complete works had just recently become available in Latin translations. He was a silent, meditative student, who devoted himself to taking notes of his master's lectures, some of which, on Aristotle's *Ethics*, survive in autograph. He was already a massive man, slow in movement and imperturbably calm: his fellow students teasingly called him 'The Dumb Ox', but they circulated his lecture-notes with admiration. Only when forced to do so by the etiquette of scholastic disputation did Thomas exhibit the astounding superiority of his dialectical talents. 'This dumb ox', said Albert on one such occasion, 'will fill the whole world with his bellowing.'

By 1252 Albert came to believe that Thomas had learnt all he had to teach him in philosophy and theology, and that he was now qualified to begin advanced studies. Hitherto Thomas's experience of study and teaching had been mainly in philosophy, though it is possible that he had assisted Albert in elementary lectures on the Bible. He was now twenty-seven, and had been a priest for two years: but by the standards of the time he was still young to begin studies for the mastership in theology. Albert convinced the Master General of the Dominicans of Thomas's wholly exceptional ability, and he was sent to Paris to proceed as Bachelor and to start giving the theological courses which qualified eventually for the Mastership. The lectures were to be given on the famous *Sentences* of Peter Lombard, an anthology, with commentary, of authoritative patristic and ecclesiastical texts. The lectures on the *Sentences* given by Thomas at Paris during the four years of preparation for the Mastership constitute the first of his major surviving works. Even in this commentary on a standard textbook he shows himself an original genius.

When Thomas went to the University of Paris, universities were still comparatively new things. In the preceding century there had grown from the Cathedral school of Notre Dame a thriving academic institution with an extensive curriculum and an international student body: its statutes as a self-governing university had been approved in the name of the Pope in 1215. Universities in Italy and Spain were also in their infancy, and about the same time Oxford and Cambridge received their first Chancellors. The oldest Oxford and Cambridge colleges were still in the future: just after Thomas was lecturing on the

Sentences in Paris the delinquent baron John de Balliol was ordered, as a penance, to found a house of scholars in Oxford. The University of Bologna specialised in law, and that of Montpellier in medicine; but the international focus of the study of philosophy and theology was, beyond compare, the University of Paris.

The Dominicans had established a house of study in Paris in 1217, and despite their unpopularity among the more traditional clergy they had obtained control, by 1230, of two of the twelve chairs of theology in the University. When Thomas arrived his role was to act as apprentice to one Elias Brunet, who had succeeded Albert the Great as holder of the junior of the two Dominican chairs in 1248. The chair was an object of great contention: in 1252 the University had attempted to suppress it, and in the course of the ensuing controversy the majority of professors went on strike for the greater part of the academic year. Thomas seems to have given his first course of lectures as a strike-breaker, and one of his chores as Bachelor was to write a refutation of anti-Dominican pamphlets.

The heart of the Paris education was the course of lectures. On most days the Professor would lecture from six o'clock in the morning until after eight; the Bachelor would then lecture on the *Sentences* from nine until shortly before noon. On special days the Professor would preside at formal disputations on topics of his choice: a problem was raised and conflicting opinions were stated and argued, the Bachelor had to respond to arguments raised by the audience, and finally judgement was given by the Master. During Lent and Advent, instead of these *Quaestiones Disputatae* on set topics, there were more wide-ranging impromptu discussions, *Quaestiones Quodlibetales*, in which any member of the audience could raise a question on any topic.

Besides lecturing and taking part in disputations Thomas while a Bachelor wrote two short monographs at the request of his Dominican colleagues: the works *On the Principles of Nature* and *On Being and Essence*. These explained the terminology of Aristotelian and post-Aristotelian physics and metaphysics respectively: both, and especially the latter, became popular as handy introductory manuals.

In the academic year 1255–6 Thomas was ordered to proceed to the degree of Master and to take up the chair in theology. He was only thirty, and was doubtful of his own competence: he might well hesitate to assume such a responsibility at a time when anti-Dominican feeling in Paris was so strong that the priory needed a guard of royal troops for twenty-four hours a day. But a dream encouraged him, and even suggested a text for his inaugural lecture; he was installed in spring 1256, amid elaborate academic ceremonial, protected by an explicit Papal prohibition against demonstrations.

For the next three years Thomas's principal academic duty was to lecture on the text of the Bible. Among the biblical commentaries which have come down to us, there probably belong to this period the commentaries on the prophet Isaiah and on the Gospel of St Matthew. The commentaries have survived in two forms: the *reportatio* or student's notes on lectures, and the *ordinatio*, or text written or dictated by the lecturer himself. The manuscripts of St Thomas are a mixed blessing for the scholar: for centuries his handwriting has been a byword for illegibility, and his autographs look like something between a shorthand and a cypher.

Aquinas's commentaries on Scripture are nowadays comparatively little read even by theologians. A more interesting memorial of his first Paris professorship is the text of the disputations over which he presided, traditionally known, from the topic of the first of them, as *Disputed Questions on Truth*. These disputations concern many different areas of philosophy and theology: truth and the knowledge of truth in God, angels and men; providence and predestination, grace and justification; reason, conscience and freewill; emotion, trances, prophecy, education, and a dozen other topics. Altogether there are twenty-nine 'questions', each of them devoted to a single theme; but each question is itself a set of many individual disputations or 'articles'. Thus, the first question, on truth, consists of no less than twelve disputations, from the first article 'What is truth?' to the twelfth 'Is there falsehood in the understanding?' Altogether there are two hundred and fifty-three articles in this Paris collection, and the total amounts to over five hundred thousand words. Thus, the *Disputed Questions on Truth*, a comparatively minor work of Aquinas, by itself amounts to more than half the total surviving output of Aristotle. The text of the disputations was made available by Paris booksellers: in 1304 it could be rented for copying, in forty-six fascicules, for four shillings.

The form and method of the disputations can be illustrated by the first article of the first question, 'What is truth?' Seven arguments are first set out to the effect that to be true is simply to be, taking as a starting point the dictum of Augustine that truth is that which is, and concluding with a discussion of a famous passage of Aristotle's *Metaphysics* on the definition of truth. There follow five arguments to the contrary, maintaining that being is not at all the same thing as being true. Then comes Aquinas's determination of the dispute, in which he distinguishes three senses of 'true' and 'truth'. Strictly speaking, truth is a relationship between the mind and reality: the conformity of a thought to what it is a thought about. But the state of affairs which makes a thought true can itself be called 'the truth': it is in that sense that the truth is that which is. Again, while an idle thought of mine may accord with reality whether or not I know it to do so, it is when I *judge* a thought to accord with reality that the notion of truth has a special application. Hence we may regard truth as in different ways belonging to reality, to thought, and to judgement. Having made this triple distinction, Aquinas goes back to the initial arguments for and against the identification of being and being true: taking them one by one, he explains what in each he regards as correct and what as incorrect. To read the text of the article aloud takes about half an hour: if our editions are anything like a verbatim record of the original proceedings, the entire disputation on truth must have lasted about five hours.

Philosophers of the present day still worry about the definition of truth, and contemporary discussions still take as their starting point Aristotle's remark in the *Metaphysics*. Corresponding to the thesis that to be true simply is to be, there is the contemporary 'redundancy theory' of truth, according to which in all sentences of the form '*p* is true' the phrase 'is true' is logically superfluous, so that to say ' "Snow is white" is true' is to say no more than 'Snow is white'. Other twentieth-century philosophers have believed, like Aquinas, that truth consists in correspondence with reality, though they have commonly taken as the primary bearers of truth – the items which do the corresponding – not thoughts or judgements but sentences or propositions. Many aspects of contemporary controversies find their counterparts in these medieval disputations: for instance, philosophers today debate whether propositions can change their 'truth-value', that is, pass from truth to falsehood or vice versa; the same problem is raised in the sixth article of the first question, 'Whether created truth is immutable'.

In addition to these structured disputations on truth and related matters, there survive from Aquinas' first Paris period also impromptu quodlibetical disputations. Some concern issues of topical polemic, as the question whether friars are obliged to perform manual labour. Others no doubt reflect the curiosity of individuals in the audience, as the question whether there are real worms in Hell. (No, said Thomas; only the gnawing of conscience.)

During these years in Paris Aquinas found time to begin, but never to finish, a commentary on a treatise on the Trinity by the sixth-century philosopher Boethius. In this unlikely place there is to be found his fullest treatment of the relationship between natural science, mathematics and metaphysics. There is a long discussion of the view that these three disciplines represent a hierarchy of increasing abstraction from matter.

In the spring of 1259 Thomas was succeeded in his chair of theology by an English Dominican, William of Alton; he left Paris shortly after and spent the next six years in Italy. At the time the Papal Court was not yet stably established in the Vatican: Alexander IV, who was Pope when Thomas returned to Italy, lived at Anagni, and his successor, Urban IV, was crowned at Viterbo and moved a year later to Orvieto. During the early 60s Thomas was to be found teaching at Orvieto, Rome and Viterbo, and mingling with the scholars, diplomats and missionaries at the Papal court. The most important achievement of the first part of this Italian sojourn was the completion of a work begun in Paris: the *Summa contra Gentiles,* the *Summary* or *Manual against the Gentiles,* known in English translation as *On the Truth of the Catholic Faith.*

The Summa contra Gentiles was an encyclopaedic theological manual for the use of missionaries among Jews and Muslims: the idea of the work seems to have been suggested by the Spanish Dominican Raymond of Peñafort who was evangelising non-Christians in Spain and North Africa. What gives the book its particular character, and its importance in the history of philosophy, is the fact that the Muslims and Jews for whose conversion it was written included men thoroughly versed in Aristotelian learning. Hence it sets out to argue from philosophical premises without sectarian presuppositions, and treats topics with a subtle sophistication quite unlike the typical style of missionary apologetic.

The *Summa contra Gentiles* is a treatise, not a record of disputations: it is in four books of a hundred or so chapters each, amounting to some three hundred thousand words in all. The first book is about the nature of God, in so far as this is held to be knowable by reason unaided by revelation; the second concerns the created world and its production by God; the third expounds the way in which rational creatures are to find their happiness in God, and thus ranges widely over ethical matters; the fourth is devoted to specifically Christian doctrines such as the Trinity, the Incarnation, the Sacraments and the final resurrection of the Saints through the power of Christ. Throughout, Aquinas scrupulously distinguishes between those truths about God and creation which he believes can be established by reasoning independent of any alleged revelation, and those which are only provable by appeal to divine authority communicated through the Bible or the teaching of the Christian Church. In the first three books Biblical and ecclesiastical texts are used only to illustrate and confirm the conclusions reached, never as premises from which the arguments start. Aquinas explains his method in the second chapter of Book I:

Mahometans and pagans do not agree with us in accepting the authority of any Scripture we might use in refuting them, in the way in which we can dispute against Jews by appeal to the Old Testament and against heretics by appeal to the New. These people accept neither. Hence we must have recourse to natural reason, to which all men are forced to assent.

Natural reason, Thomas believed, was capable of reaching only a limited number of truths about God: doctrines such as the Trinity and the Incarnation were known only by revelation and unprovable by unaided reason. Even those truths which were in theory open to reason, such as the existence of God and the immortality of the soul, must in practice be accepted by many people on authority; to establish them by philosophical argument demands more intelligence, leisure and energy than can be expected from the majority of mankind.

Having drawn the boundaries between reason and faith, Aquinas considers what reason has to say about the existence of God. Some say this doctrine needs no proof: 'God exists' is a self-evident truth since anyone who understands what the word 'God' means must see that there is a God. Attempts to prove the existence of God from the definition of 'God' have indeed been made by philosophers from St Anselm in the century before Aquinas right up to the present day. Aquinas himself rejected such attempts; the belief that God's existence is self-evident, he says, results mainly from people's being accustomed to hear talk about God since their earliest childhood. Not being self-evident, God's existence needs proof: and Aquinas offers two lengthy and difficult proofs drawn from Aristotle's *Physics*. He goes on to prove various truths about God's nature: God is eternal, unchanging, immaterial and free from all composition. These truths, he insists, are all essentially negative; they tell us what God is *not* like, they do not give us any genuine insight into his nature.

We can however say some positive things about God, provided that we understand clearly what we are doing when we form sentences with 'God' as their subject. The words by which we describe God and creatures are not used in the same sense about each. (Similarly, to adapt one of Aquinas' examples, we do not mean quite the same thing when we call the sun 'bright' as when we call the colour of a patch of paint 'bright'.) On the other hand, if we say that God is wise and that Socrates is wise, we are not making a mere pun. In Aquinas's technical terminology, when we talk of God's goodness, or his wisdom, or his love, we are using words not univocally, or equivocally, but *analogically*. Using language thus analogically, we can say many things about God: we can speak of his universal knowledge of all truth, all individuals, and all events past present or future; and we can speak of his free and sovereign will and his love of himself and of his creatures. The major part of Book I of the *Summa contra Gentiles* is devoted to establishing such analogical truths about God's intellect and will.

Book II treats of another of God's attributes: his omnipotence. It discusses the sense in which God can be said to be able to do everything even though he cannot die or change or weary or undo the past or create another God. The book is mainly concerned not with the attributes of God in himself, but with God's relation to the world. It elaborates the thesis that God created the world out of nothing: a doctrine not to be found in Aristotle but derived historically from Jewish and Christian reflection on the Book of Genesis. Aquinas believed that reason could show that the world had been created but not that the world had had a beginning in time. The world might, for all unaided reason could show, have existed for ever. It would still be a creature of God in the sense that it was permanently dependent on him for its existence and was not made out of any material whose existence was independent of his good pleasure.

Aristotle had believed that he could show that the cosmos has existed from all eternity: since the Catholic faith taught that the world had had a beginning in time, there must be something wrong, St Thomas thought, with the reasons offered to prove its eternity – and he devotes seven dense chapters (31–7) to refuting them. On the other hand it is a mistake, he thinks, to try to prove by argument that the world *did* have a beginning in time – and he devotes a chapter to the refutation of arguments offered on that side. He then turns from the creation of the world (the question 'Why are there things at all?') to what he calls the 'distinction' of the world (the question 'Why are there the particular kinds of things that there are?'). He criticises various more or less evolutionary accounts of the origin of species; the distinctions to be found in the world, he claims, are due to a deliberate intention of God to make the created universe as hierarchically perfect as possible.

Much of Book II is devoted to the topic of 'intellectual substances': angels and human souls. Aquinas identifies the extra-terrestrial intelligences to which Greek philosophers had attributed the causation of astronomical phenomena with the angels or messengers of God which are mentioned from time to time in the Bible. These are immaterial, incorruptible, living and free creatures which are not united to any body. Human souls are likewise spiritual and immortal, but they are individually united to individual bodies. The soul is not simply clothed with a body, nor imprisoned in a body: it is the 'form' of the body, that is to say, it is what makes the body a living body of the kind it is, rather as the shape of a key is what makes it the key of a particular door, or the pitch of a note what makes it the particular note it is.

Animals too, for Aquinas, have souls, and so do plants; but unlike human souls, these principles of life are not immortal or separable from their bodies. Though human beings grow like plants and feed and breed like animals, human beings do not have vegetable and animal souls as well as their immortal soul: there is one single form in a human being which is his intellectual soul.

At this point Aquinas devotes much energy to controverting Arabic interpretations of Aristotle according to which there is only one single intellect for the whole human race, an intellect independent of and distinct from the souls of individual human beings. It is important for St Thomas to maintain that the highest intellectual human faculties are part of the equipment of the individual human soul, because it is to the intellectual powers of the soul that he appeals when, in the final section of the book, he comes to offer proof of the immortality of the individual soul. Though immortal, the human soul does not exist before the origin of the human body to which it belongs. Nor is it inherited from parents, as bodily features are: it is not transmitted with the semen, but is a fresh creation by God in the case of each human being.

The third book begins with a consideration of good and evil. God is the supreme good, and the cause of all other goodness: but there is no supreme evil. Evils are in a manner uncaused, because they are not realities in the same way as good things are; the creatures whose defects constitute evil are caused by God. All things exist for the sake of God; God is their end or goal. Intelligent and non-intelligent creatures alike, in so far as they develop in accordance with their natures, mirror divine goodness; in addition, intelligent creatures find their fulfilment in the understanding and contemplation of God. Human happiness is not to be found in sensual pleasures, in honour, glory, riches or worldly power, nor in the exercise of skill or moral virtue; it is to be found in the knowledge of God, not as he can be known in this life by human conjecture, tradition or argument, but in the vision of the divine essence which Aquinas believes he can show to be possible in another life by means of supernatural divine enlightenment. Chapters 50–63 treat of this beatific vision: its nearest equivalent in the present life is the philosophical contemplation in which Aristotle alleged happiness to consist.

A lengthy treatment of divine providence and its effects throughout the hierarchy of created beings leads to a detailed discussion of the relationship between the course of the heavenly bodies and the events of human life. Aquinas does not deny that heavenly bodies may affect human conduct – after all, a hot sun may decide me to take off my overcoat – but he insists that they do not do so in such a way as to determine human choice and make possible a science of astrology. Magic, however, is possible: but magicians operate not by the power of the stars, but by the aid of demons, who are sinful angels.

Aquinas next introduces, with surprising brevity, the notion of a divine law which obliges us to love God and our neighbour, to accept the true faith and offer worship. He devotes five chapters to sexual ethics: the sinfulness of fornication and contraception; the indissolubility of marriage and the necessity of monogamy; the impermissibility of incest. He next offers a vigorous dis-cussion of voluntary poverty – a clear echo of the Paris con-troversies.

The book ends with a treatment of reward and punishment, divine and human, and of the need for grace, or supernatural divine assistance, if a man is to be freed from sin and persevere in virtue. Those who so persevere and achieve their final goal have been predestined by God from all eternity; and those who through sin fail to achieve happiness have been eternally repro-bated. This necessity of grace and predestination if a man is to reach final happiness is regarded as something which can be proved, given sufficient wit, time and goodwill, by natural reason. It is only in the fourth book that Aquinas turns to those doctrines which he believes are beyond the reach of the human intellect and are articles of faith.

The fourth book is divided into three parts which correspond to the first three books. As Book I dealt with what reason can tell of God's own nature, the first part of Book IV deals with what faith reveals about God's own life: the doctrine of the Trinity. Book II dealt with God's activity in the created world: the second part of Book IV deals with the doctrine of the Incar-nation according to which God entered into the created world by taking flesh in Jesus Christ. Book III dealt with the goal of human life and the way to reach that goal by obedience to natural law; the final part of Book IV concerns the resurrection of the body in glory, and the sacraments of the Church which are designed to help sinners on their journey to heaven.

In the *Summa contra Gentiles* Aquinas shows a very comprehensive knowledge of Aristotle. In the course of writing the work he became aware of the unsatisfactory nature of many of the Latin versions of his works then current. In 1261, at Orvieto in the court of Urban IV, he came across the new and excellent translation of Aristotle's treatises on animals by the Flemish Dominican William of Moerbeke. He hastened to make use of it in his text; and at his instigation Moerbeke during the next decade produced improved translations of the majority of Aristotle's works. It was on the basis of Moerbeke's revisions that Aquinas was later to write his own commentaries on Aristotle. He was himself ignorant of Greek, but he was constrained by the ecumenical interests of Urban IV to familiarise himself with the writings of Greek theologians and the acts of Greek ecclesiastical councils. These researches have left traces in the final part of the first *Summa* and were embodied in a monograph entitled *Against the Errors of the Greeks* written at Urban's request. Other quotations from Greek authorities were woven into a continuous commentary on the Gospels, built up from Patristic quotations, which Thomas began for Urban and which occupied him for several years after the Pope's death. Known as the *Catena Aurea* or *Golden Chain*, it has been described as an almost perfect conspectus of Patristic interpretation.

According to tradition, Thomas was employed by Urban IV as a writer of prayers and hymns. In 1264 the Pope instituted the new feast of Corpus Christi in honour of the sacrament of the eucharist in which, according to Catholic belief, bread and wine were changed into the body and blood of Christ. The three hymns which Thomas wrote for the office of the feast have been popular among Roman Catholics ever since. Thomas's poetry is a remarkable combination of theological technicalities of a highly scholastic kind with scholarly biblical allusiveness and religious emotion tersely and vividly expressed. The sequence of the Corpus Christi mass, the *Lauda Sion,* has a jerky vigour quite unlike the passionless lucidity of his theological prose. Another of Aquinas's eucharistic hymns, *Adoro te Devote,* was to be translated by Gerard Manley Hopkins into equally lively English. One verse runs:

Seeing, touching, tasting are in thee deceived;
How says trusty hearing? that shall be believed;
What God's Son hath told me, take for truth I do;
Truth himself speaks truly or there's nothing true.

None of Aquinas's admirers would claim him as a great poet: but his poetry contrasts so sharply with his prose works that it should be read by anyone who wishes to see his character as a whole.*

In 1265, after the death of Pope Urban, Aquinas was sent to Rome to open a house of studies for Dominicans. He spent two years teaching theology at Santa Sabina, one of the most beautiful and most beautifully situated churches of the city. The most substantial fruit of his work at Rome is a series of ten disputed questions, named from the first of them *On the Power of God.* The first six of these questions cover, in greater depth, the problems about omnipotence and creation raised in the second book of the *Summa contra Gentiles*; the remaining four concern topics in Trinitarian doctrine which were points of conflict between Greek and Latin theologians. The longest and most interesting disputation is the third question, of nineteen articles, on creation.

Though these questions *On the Power of God* represent a maturer thought than those *On Truth* they are less lively and interesting. This is no doubt a reflection of a difference between the audience at the foremost university in the world and the audience in a humble provincial house of studies. To the same period there belongs possibly another series of disputed questions, *On Evil*. Both these series of questions to some extent anticipate the thought of St Thomas's final masterpiece, the *Summa Theologiae* or *Summary of Theology*: the questions on power correspond to the first part of the *Summa*, and the questions on the seven deadly sins correspond to parts of the second part.

* St Thomas seems to have originated, perhaps inadvertently, a novel verse form: the limerick. A prayer of thanksgiving which he wrote contains the following lines:

Sit vitiorum meorum evacuatio
Concupiscentiae et libidinis exterminatio
Caritatis et patientiae
Humilitatis et obedientiae
Omniumque virtutum augmentatio.

The *Summa* itself seems to have been begun as a result of St Thomas's teaching experience in Rome. It was designed as a textbook for beginners in theology to replace the *Sentences* of Peter Lombard. To the modern reader it appears rather alarming as an introductory text, not only because of its size – incomplete though it is, it runs to over two million words – but also because of its elaborate format and technical terminology. It is something between a treatise and a set of disputed questions. Like a disputation, it is divided into questions and articles, not into chapters, but the multiple arguments for and against a particular thesis which introduce a genuine disputation are replaced by an introductory triad of difficulties against the position which Aquinas intends to take up in the body of the article. These objections are followed, usually, by a single, almost ceremonial, argument for the other side beginning with the words 'But on the other hand ... ' and usually consisting in the citation of an authoritative text. It is after this, in the main body of the article, that Aquinas sets out his own position with the reasons that support it. Each article then concludes with the solution of the difficulties set out in the introductory objections.

The *Summa* is, in its way, a masterpiece of philosophical style. The practice of beginning each topic with the three strongest arguments that came to mind against the position to be defended must have served as a marvellous discipline to the author. Certainly it provides a fascinating stimulus to the reader. Once one has become accustomed to the syntax of medieval Latin and the technicalities of scholastic jargon – which were not, of course, the invention of Thomas but current coin when he wrote – one finds the style smooth, lucid, civil and judicious. In writing of abstruse metaphysical matters Aquinas sometimes falls into confusion; but he almost never lapses into rhetoric.

Of the three gigantic parts into which the *Summa* is divided only the first was written in Italy: it was most probably finished in Viterbo, shortly after Aquinas rejoined the Papal court in 1267. Most of the 119 articles of the first part cover the same ground as Books I and II of the *Summa contra Gentiles*: but since the readers now in mind are Catholic students of theology rather than potential converts from Mohammedanism or Jewry, St Thomas can expound the doctrine of the Trinity in the treatise on the divine nature rather than segregating it to a separate book on mysteries of faith. But he remains careful to distinguish between truths of natural theology accessible to reason and mysteries communicated only by revelation and credible only by supernatural faith.

The first part of the *Summa* is more economical and at the same time clearer and richer than the corresponding parts of the *Summa contra Gentiles*. Thus, for instance, the two Aristotelian proofs of the existence of God in the earlier work are replaced by the clearer, brisker, and more famous Five Ways which, on the surface at least, are less closely dependent on Greek astronomical speculation. Again, the treatise on human nature which occupies questions 75–102 of the later *Summa* is much fuller and more systematic than the corresponding section in the second book of the earlier work, and it is proportionately less heavily loaded with criticism of Arabian exegesis of Aristotle's psychology. Not that Aquinas had lost interest in Aristotle: far from it, he constantly drew on his ideas and made prompt use of the treatises and commentaries that were being translated by William of Moerbeke at Viterbo.

While writing the first part of the *Summa* St Thomas began a political treatise, entitled *On Kingship* and dedicated to a mysterious, and possibly non-existent, King Henry of Cyprus. Written in the Pope's domain while the Popes were putting themselves under the protection of the French royal family to ward off the threat of the Hohenstaufen Emperors and their kin, it lays down principles for the guidance of temporal governors in a way which leaves no doubt that kings are subject to priests and that the Pope enjoys a secular as well as a spiritual supremacy. The work was left unfinished when St Thomas died, and was completed after his death by the historian Tolomeo of Lucca.

During this period at Viterbo, Aquinas was offered, and declined, the archbishopric of Naples. In 1268 he was sent back to the chair he had formerly held in Paris, where a fresh attack was being made on the unpopular friars, and where an ultra-Aristotelian movement was bringing into disrepute the type of synthesis between Aristotle and Christianity that was attempted in such works as the two *Summa*s.

In Paris Aquinas's duties as professor involved, as before, lecturing on the Bible and presiding at scholastic disputations. He seems to have lectured at this period on the Gospel of St John and on the Pauline Epistles: the commentary on St Paul's epistle to the Romans, which he prepared for publication himself, is more widely read than most of his scriptural writings. Shortly after his arrival he presided over disputations recorded in the *Disputed Questions on the Soul*. Later disputations from this second period in Paris concerned the 'theological virtues' of hope and charity, and the 'cardinal virtues' of prudence, temperance, fortitude and justice. These latter disputations concerned topics which were the subject-matter of the second part of the *Summa*. Every Advent and Lent, as before, Aquinas held quodlibetical disputations on various questions of topical interest: quodlibets 1–6 and 12 are generally attributed to this period. The first set, dating from Lent 1269, include such questions as whether monks are bound to be vegetarians, whether sacramental confession of sins can be made in writing, and whether an angel can pass from one point to another without going through points between.

During the same period Aquinas wrote two pieces of defensive polemic against critics of religious orders such as the Dominicans. In particular, he defends the admission of boys to the religious life in advance of puberty, a practice which had been the subject of severe attack. Of greater interest to philosophical readers, however, are the other polemical works of this period, written in defence of Christian Aristotelianism.

Aristotle's logic had been studied in Latin universities ever since there had been universities: but his physical and metaphysical writings long remained an object of suspicion to ecclesiastical academic authorities. The statutes of Paris in 1215, indeed, had forbidden professors in the Faculty of Arts to lecture on them at all. The condemnation was reinforced by Papal bulls in 1231 and 1263, but seems to have become a dead letter by the middle of the century; indeed in 1255 the Faculty of Arts made the study of all the known works of Aristotle obligatory on its members.

During Aquinas's first professorship in Paris the use of Aristotle's metaphysics had thus been a prerogative of theologians like himself; but by the time of his return it was the professional philosophers of the Faculty of Arts who were the foremost exponents of Aristotelianism. These philosophical

Aristotelians were not as cautious as the theologians had been in toning down or disowning those Aristotelian theses which clashed with Christian doctrine. Two topics which were arousing the most lively conflict around 1270 were the individuation of the intellect and the eternity of the world.

In Aristotelian psychology, as expounded in Aristotle's *De Anima* (*On the Soul*) and the commentaries written on it by Greek and Arabic scholars, there are three different items which correspond in different ways to what we in English call 'the mind'. The mind as the object of introspection was known as the imagination or fancy; the mind as the storehouse of ideas and the locus of the acquired intellectual skills was known as the receptive intellect; the mind as the power to abstract intellectual information from sensory experience was known as the active intellect. The relationship between these three entities is left obscure by Aristotle. Aquinas, as we have seen, interpreted the theory in the *Summa contra Gentiles* in such a way that not only the imagination but also the potential and the active intellects are powers or faculties of individual human beings. The Arabic philosopher Ibn Sina or Avicenna (980–1037) had maintained that there was only one active intellect for the whole human race. Some Christians were happy to accept this, identifying the active intellect with that divine illumination of the human mind which had been eloquently described by St Augustine. But the philosopher Ibn Rushd or Averroes (1126–98) taught that not only the active intellect but also the receptive intellect was something which was shared by the human race as a whole instead of being the possession of each individual. When this version of Aristotelian psychology was taught in the Faculty of Arts in Paris it brought its proponents into conflict with the ecclesiastical authorities, since it appeared to undermine belief in personal immortality.

The theory of a single common intellect is only doubtfully attributable to Aristotle; but there is no doubt of the authenticity of the second contentious doctrine, the eternity of the world. In the *Summa contra Gentiles*, as we have seen, Aquinas had been careful to dissociate himself from this doctrine: but the Aristotelians in the Faculty of Arts in the 1260s were willing to defend it. They were attacked by a young Franciscan theologian, John Pecham, later to be Archbishop of Canterbury, who maintained that reason could show that there was a time when God existed and the world did not.

St Thomas had to defend his own moderate Aristotelianism from attacks on both fronts. Against the admirers of Averroes he wrote a tract *On the Unity of the Intellect*: by detailed exegesis of Aristotle's text and his commentators' glosses, and by a battery of philosophical arguments, he demolished the theory of a single receptive intellect. In defence of Aristotle, however, and against Pecham, he wrote *On the Eternity of the World* to argue that there is no contradiction in the theory that the world had no beginning. That creation took place at a particular point in time is something to be accepted on faith, not demonstrated by reason.

These two treatises were written in 1269 or 1270. On 10 December 1270 the Archbiship of Paris condemned a list of thirteen doctrines beginning with the proposition 'The intellect of all men is one and numerically the same' and including the propositions 'The world is eternal' and 'There never was a first man'. None of the condemned propositions represented doctrines which Aquinas had ever taught; and with the exception of these propositions the teaching of Aristotle was no longer impugned.

The greatest of Thomas's services to Aristotelianism during these years was the remarkable series of commentaries on the works of Aristotle which he seems to have written between 1269 and 1273. Two of the earliest were those on the *De anima* and the *Physics*, the two Aristotelian works directly relevant to the controversies about the soul and the world's eternity. The controversies seem to have convinced Thomas that the best antidote to heterodox Aristotelianism was a thorough knowledge of the entire Aristotelian system. So he wrote line-by-line commentaries on two of Aristotle's logical works (the *De Interpretatione* and the *Posterior Analytics*), on the entire *Nicomachean Ethics* and on twelve books of the *Metaphysics*. At his death he left unfinished commentaries on half-a-dozen other works of Aristotle including the *De Caelo* and the *Politics*.

Had these commentaries on Aristotle been all that Aquinas left behind him, they would have been enough to show that he was a philosopher of extraordinary power and industry. Because they are based on an imperfect translation of defective manuscripts, they have to a great extent been superseded by others written since the flowering of philological studies in the nineteenth century; but there are many obscure passages in Aristotle's works on which to this day a consultation of Aquinas throws light. The commentaries are everywhere lucid, intelligent and sympathetic: and the half-million words of the commentary on the *Metaphysics* constitute a philosophical classic in its own right. The value of these commentaries by a theologian was soon appreciated by the philosophers of the Paris Arts faculty. Though Thomas had championed the rights of theology against the heterodox Aristotelians, it was the Faculty of Arts, and not that of Theology, that petitioned the Dominican authorities for his recall when he left Paris for the last time in 1672.

Of all the writings of St Thomas during his second Paris professorship the best known is not any of those so far mentioned, but the second part of the *Summa Theologiae*. This, which is by far the longest of the three parts, is always further divided in editions: the first part of the second part (*Prima Secundae*, cited always as 'Ia IIae' or – as in this book – 'I–II') and the second part of the second part (*Secunda Secundae*, IIa IIae or II–II). This corresponds in subject-matter to the third book of the earlier *Summa*: but it marks a much greater advance on it than the first part does on the first two books of that work. It is best described as a Christian treatise on ethics, and its structure is modelled on the *Nicomachean Ethics* on which Aquinas was at the same time writing his commentary.

The *Nicomachean Ethics* aims to portray the good life for man: the life of happiness or *eudaimonia*. Happiness, according to Aristotle, is the activity of the soul in accordance with virtue: as there are two parts of the soul, intellectual and emotional, so there are two kinds of virtue, intellectual and moral. Virtue, whether intellectual or moral, is a psychic disposition which finds expression in voluntary action, and in particular in actions deliberately chosen as part of a worked-out plan of life. Moral virtue is expressed in the choice and pursuit of a middle course between excessive and deficient emotion and exaggerated or inadequate action: this is the famous doctrine of the golden mean, according to which each virtue stands in the middle flanked by opposing vices. Thus, courage or fortitude is a mean between cowardice and rashness; temperance is a mean between profligacy and insensibility. Justice, the most important of the moral virtues, is also concerned with a mean in the sense that it aims at each man's getting neither more nor less than his due: but it is not, like the other virtues, flanked by opposing vices since any departure from the just mean, on either side, involves simply injustice. Moral virtue prevents disordered emotion from leading to inappropriate action. What decides, in any given case, what *is* the appropriate action and the correct amount of feeling is the intellectual virtue of prudence or practical wisdom (*phronesis*): this is the virtue of that part of the reason which is concerned with action. The virtue of the speculative part of the reaction is learning, or philosophic wisdom (*sophia*): this virtue finds its most sublime manifestation in more or less solitary contemplation (*theoria*). The supreme happiness, according to the *Ethics*, consists in a life of philosophical contemplation: but though this is the best life for man, it is also in a sense a superhuman life. A secondary kind of happiness can be found in a life of political activity and public magnificence in accordance with the moral virtues.

Aquinas found in the *Nicomachean Ethics* much that was congenial to the Christian moral thinking of his time – some of which indeed derived, by various indirect routes, from the ethical theories of Plato and Aristotle and other Greek thinkers. Some of the more repellent pagan features of the work he modified or, as he would put it, 'benignly interpreted'. Some other Aristotelian features he incorporated so successfully into his synthesis that to some of his later Catholic admirers they came to seem home-grown features of Christianity.

The *Prima Secundae* begins, like the *Nicomachean Ethics*, by considering the ultimate end or goal of human life. Like Aristotle Aquinas identifies the ultimate end with happiness, and like him he thinks that happiness cannot be equated with pleasure, riches, honour or any bodily good, but must consist in activity in accordance with virtue, especially intellectual virtue. The intellectual activity which satisfies the Aristotelian requirements for happiness is to be found perfectly only in contemplation of the essence of God; happiness in the ordinary conditions of the present life must remain imperfect. True happiness, then, even on Aristotle's terms, is to be found only in the souls of the blessed in Heaven. The Saints will in due course receive a bonus of happiness, undreamt of by Aristotle, in the resurrection of the body in glory.

Aristotle, in the course of defining virtue, was drawn into a discussion of the nature of human voluntary action; the more systematic Aquinas prefaces his discussion of virtue with a full treatise on action and a full treatise on emotion. Questions 6 to 17 concern the nature of action: they analyse concepts such as voluntariness, intention, choice, deliberation, action and desire, with a thoroughness which represents a great advance on Aristotle. They constitute a philosophical treatment of the nature of the human will which bears comparison with anything written on the topic ever since. At question 18 Aquinas turns from philosophical psychology to moral philosophy: he asks what makes a human action a good action or a bad action. Questions 18 to 21 are the kernel of his ethics: taken together with the treatment of virtue in questions 49–50 they set out the framework into which the discussion of particular moral topics is inserted. Virtue, according to Aristotle, concerns not only action but also feelings: accordingly, questions 22 to 48 are devoted to a consideration of the emotions, or passions of the soul. This part of the *Summa* is not much read nowadays: but it goes into greater detail and betrays greater insight in many places than the better known treatises on the passions by Descartes and Hume.

Since virtue in the Aristotelian definition is a psychic disposition, Aquinas introduces his theory of virtue with a long disquisition on the nature of dispositions, questions 49–54. This is an original philosophical investigation of great importance, which works into an articulate system incidental remarks of Aristotle and of his commentators. The importance of the study of human dispositions (*habitus*) was lost sight of with the decline of scholastic philosophy at the Renaissance, and was rediscovered only in our own time by linguistic philosophers such as Wittgenstein and Ryle.

The account of the nature of virtue itself, of the distinction between moral and intellectual virtues, and of the relation between virtue and emotion, follows Aristotle more closely. But then Aquinas introduces an entirely Christian topic: the study of the theological virtues of faith, hope, and charity, listed as a trio by St Paul and given a commanding role in patristic tradition. The Aristotelian virtues are compared and contrasted with these Scriptural virtues (questions 62–7), with the gifts of the spirit of God mentioned in a familiar passage of Isaiah (68) and with the virtues singled out by Christ for commendation in the beatitudes of the Sermon on the Mount (69). Having linked Aristotelian virtues with the gifts of character prized in Christian tradition, Aquinas next proceeds to connect Aristotelian vices with Scriptural concepts of sin. Nineteen questions are devoted to sin: a section which is much more theological and much less philosophical than the first part of the *Prima Secundae*.

The two final sections of the *Prima Secundae* are devoted to law and grace. Questions 90–108 constitute a theologico-philosophical treatise on jurisprudence: the nature of law; the distinction between natural and positive law; the source and extent of the powers of human legislators; the contrast between the divine laws of the Old and of the New Testament. From question 109 until the end at question 114 Aquinas treats of the nature of divine grace and the necessity of grace for salvation. The *Prima Secundae* concludes with a brief treatise on the justification of sinners, the topic which at the time of the Reformation divided Catholics and Lutherans.

If the *Prima Secundae* is the General Part of Aquinas's ethics, the *Secunda Secundae* contains his detailed teaching on individual moral topics. He takes each virtue in turn and analyses its nature, then lists the sins which conflict with it. First the theological virtues and the corresponding sins are discussed: the virtue of faith and the sins of unbelief, heresy and apostasy; the virtue of hope and the sins of despair and presumption; the virtue of charity and the sins of hatred, envy, discord and sedition. It is in the section on the sins against faith that Aquinas sets out his views on the persecution of heretics, and it is in the section on the sins against charity that he sets out the conditions under which the making of war is justified (questions 10–11 and 40 respectively).

With the treatment of prudence (47–56) and justice (57–80) we return to the Aristotelian framework. The treatise on justice is far fuller and richer than anything to be found in Aristotle; it deals with the majority of the topics that would nowadays be covered by a textbook of criminal law: homicide, theft, unjust enrichment, injuries against the person, fraud, slander, usury, misconduct by judges and advocates. The discussion is always acute, lively, concrete and magisterial.

In the Aristotelian tradition the virtue of piety is often regarded as akin to, or as part of, justice: it is giving God his due. So in the *Secunda Secundae* the treatise on justice is followed by one on piety or religion. The virtue of religion is discussed in a score of questions which range over many topics from prayer and the payment of tithes to simony and necromancy. From 106 to 121 we are introduced to a number of minor virtues from Aristotle's *Ethics*: candour, gratefulness, affability, liberality: all these, it seems, are regarded by Aquinas as parts of the cardinal virtue of justice. The third cardinal virtue of courage, or fortitude, follows: it provides an opportunity for the discussion of martyrdom, magnanimity and magnificence. The final cardinal virtue is temperance, the heading under which are discussed moral questions concerned with food, drink and sex.

The Christian virtue of humility is introduced into this context, in rather strange company with the Aristotelian alleged virtues of magnanimity and magnificence enrolled under the banner of fortitude. The treatment of the contrary vice of pride gives an opportunity to touch on the sin of the first human beings, Adam and Eve. The succeeding questions, on prophecy, might be thought to be of interest only to theologians, and fundamentalist theologians at that; in fact they contain some of Aquinas's most interesting philosophical remarks on the relationship between mental imagery, propositional thought and judgement. The *Secunda Secundae* concludes, as did the *Nicomachean Ethics*, with a comparison between the active and contemplative life, to the advantage of the latter: the whole is, of course, transposed into a Christian key, and leads into a final section on the status of bishops and the life of the religious orders.

The second part of the *Summa* is Aquinas's greatest work. Its foundations and its structure are Aristotelian, and many individual sections are heavily dependent on earlier Christian thinkers: but considered as a whole it is – even from a purely philosophical viewpoint – a great advance on Aristotle. It is unsurpassed by any other Christian writer, and it retains a great deal of its interest and validity for those who live in a secular, post-Christian age.

Aquinas's second Parisian professorship was a period of amazing productivity. The *Secunda Pars* is over a million words long. To write it in three years must have required an average daily stint of a thousand words. In our century a full-time writer

would preen himself on such a regular output of highly argu-
mentative, quotation-packed, well-polished prose. But Aquinas,
while writing the *Summa*, had the duties of a full-time professor
in addition to those of a devout friar, and wrote commentaries on
the great part of the gigantic Aristotelian corpus. When one
reviews the sheer bulk of his output between 1269 and 1273 one
can believe the testimony of his chief secretary that it was his
habit, like a grand master at a chess tournament, to dictate to
three or four secretaries simultaneously; one can almost believe
the further testimony that he could dictate coherent prose while
he slept.

In the spring of 1272 Thomas left Paris to attend a general
assembly of Dominican friars at Florence. There he was given
the task of setting up a new house of theological studies for the
Dominicans in Italy. He chose to attach it to the Priory of San
Domenico in Naples, and it was there that he did his last academic work. His lectures were subsidised by the King of Naples,
Charles of Anjou, whose brother St Louis IX had learnt to appreciate his genius in Paris. Besides lecturing he was occupied
principally in completing the commentary on the *Metaphysics*
and working on the third part of the *Summa*.

The *Tertia Pars* is concerned with strictly theological topics:
twenty-six questions on the doctrine of the Incarnation, four on
the Virgin Mary, twenty-nine on the life of Christ, thirty on the
sacraments of baptism, confirmation, eucharist and penance. A
student of Aquinas's philosophy, however, would be very ill-
advised to ignore this part of his work: the discussion of the
Incarnation gives opportunity for reflection on the philosophical
problems of personal identity and individuation, and contains
remarks on predication which are still of interest to the philosopher of logic. St Thomas's presentation of the doctrine of
transubstantiation in his treatise on the Eucharist has had a great
influence on the history of theology: it also contains the fruit of
his mature philosophical thought on the nature of material substance and substantial change.

The *Summa Theologiae* was never finished. As he grew older
Aquinas was subject to fits of abstraction, as several stories attest.
At a banquet, sitting next to King Louis IX, he was oblivious of
the other guests, reflecting on theological topics, until he brought
his fist down on the table exclaiming that he had found an

argument to confute the Manichean heresy. (The courteous King sent for his secretary to take down the argument quickly before it was forgotten.) Similarly, in Naples, he had not a word to say to a Cardinal Legate who had travelled far to see him until the accompanying prelate tugged at his gown to bring him back to his senses. Finally, while saying Mass on 6 December 1273 he had a mysterious experience, which some have interpreted as a vision and some as a mental breakdown, which put an end to all his scholarly activity. He never wrote or dictated anything again, and when his secretary urged him to continue work on the *Summa*, he replied 'I cannot, because all that I have written now seems like straw.'

Early in the following year Pope Gregory X called a general council of the Church to meet at Lyons. The principal item on the agenda was the reconciliation of the Greek and Latin Churches, and Thomas, as an expert on Greek theology, was summoned to attend. Though in poor health, he set out on the journey northward; but an accidental injury to his head forced him to stop at his niece's castle near Fossanova. After some weeks he was carried into the neighbouring Cistercian monastery, where he died on 7 March 1274.

Besides the Third Part Aquinas left unfinished a number of other works on which he had worked at Naples: a commentary on the Psalms, which reaches only to the fifty-fourth Psalm, and a compendium of theology, dedicated to his secretary, which is almost a pocket edition of the *Summa*. Modern editions of the *Summa* end with a supplement, treating of the remaining sacraments of penance, anointing, marriage and order, and of the 'four last things' – death, judgement, hell and heaven: this supplement was compiled by Aquinas's secretaries from passages in his earlier writings, especially the commentary on Peter Lombard.

Within three years of his death, a number of Aquinas's opinions were publicly condemned by the authorities in the universities of Paris and Oxford; an English friar who travelled to Rome to appeal against the Oxford sentence was condemned to perpetual silence by the new Franciscan Pope Nicholas IV and died of a broken heart at Bologna. It was some fifty years before Aquinas's writings became generally regarded as theologically sound. The Paris condemnation was not revoked until 1325, two years after Thomas had been canonised as a Saint. The Oxford condemnation, so far as I know, has never been revoked.

It was in 1316 that Pope John XXII began the process of canonisation of Thomas. Very few miracles were attributed to him by the witnesses who appeared. One story, however, was attested by many eye-witnesses. When Thomas lay dying near Fossanova, they said, he had been unable to eat for days, when suddenly he expressed a wish for herrings. Herrings, his family explained, might be easy to come by in Paris, but were not to be found in the Italian seas. But to everyone's surprise, the next consignment of sardines from the local fishmonger was found to contain a load of herrings. The judges in the canonisation process seem to have been sceptical whether their untravelled witnesses would be able to tell a herring when they saw one. But the paucity of miracles did not impede the canonisation. 'There are as many miracles as there are articles of the *Summa*,' the Pope is reputed to have said; and he declared Thomas a Saint on 21 July 1323.

Even after his canonisation Aquinas did not enjoy the special prestige among Catholic theologians which he has enjoyed during most of the present century. His works have always been the subject of especial study and veneration among the Dominican scholars of his own order; but it was not until the encyclical letter *Aeterni Patris* of Pope Leo XIII in the nineteenth century that he was made, as it were, the official theologian of the whole Roman Catholic church. In 1914 Thomistic philosophy as well as Thomistic theology was given by Pius X a unique place of honour in ecclesiastical educational institutions; twenty-four Thomistic theses were listed as reliable and safe to teach in Catholic schools.

Aquinas is little read nowadays by professional philosophers: he has received much less attention in philosophy departments, whether in the continental tradition or in the Anglo-American one, than lesser thinkers such as Berkeley or Hegel. He has, of course, been extensively studied in theological colleges and in the philosophy courses of ecclesiastical institutions; but ecclesiastical endorsement has itself damaged Aquinas's reputation with secular philosophers, who have tended to discount him as simply a propagandist for Catholicism. Moreover, the official respect accorded to Aquinas by the Church has meant that his opinions and arguments have frequently been presented in crude ways by admirers who failed to appreciate his philosophical sophistication. But since the Second Vatican Council Aquinas seems to have lost something of the pre-eminent favour he enjoyed in ecclesiastical circles, and to have been superseded, in the reading-lists of ordinands, by fashionable authors judged more relevant to the contemporary scene. This wind of ecclesiastical change may blow no harm to his reputation in secular circles.

There have also been more respectable, philosophical, reasons for the neglect of Aquinas by academic philosophers; and in recent years there has been a shift in the philosophical climate also. Since Descartes the attention of philosophers had been focused on epistemology, that is to say, the attempt to make a disciplined progress from an initial sceptical position, where everything is open to doubt, to a structure of scientific thought; to construct a world of external objects and other minds from an initial deliverance or 'datum' ('given') of private and inner experience. Aquinas's epistemological interests were slight, however large epistemology might loom in 'Thomistic' philosophical textbooks, and this contributed to the contempt in which he was often held.

The assumptions of post-Cartesian philosophy have often been criticised, for instance by Marx and Freud; but it was not until the present century, with the work of the philosopher Ludwig Wittgenstein, that they were definitively undermined from within philosophy itself. Wittgenstein showed that the descriptions of private experience which the Cartesian epistemologist takes as a datum are much more problematic than the public, communal disciplines and institutions which he attempts to justify and set on sound foundations. If Wittgenstein was right, philosophy had been on a wrong tack since the time of Descartes and should alter course in a way which would make it more sympathetic to medieval preoccupations. It is not an accident that a number of those philosophers in the Anglo-American tradition who have written most sympathetically about Aquinas in recent years have been pupils of Wittgenstein.

Like Wittgenstein, the Oxford philosopher Gilbert Ryle did much to break down the barriers which had prevented modern philosophers from achieving a just appreciation of their medieval predecessors. He did so not so much by his attacks on the Cartesian separation of mind from matter – in place of which he sometimes offered a crude and unappealing identification of mind and behaviour – as by his reinstatement of the Aristotelian notions of actuality and potentiality. These philosophical concepts, and the ramified refinements of them in the Middle Ages, had been objects of mockery to philosophers and amateurs of philosophy since the time of Descartes and Molière. Ryle rediscovered or reinvented the Aristotelian distinctions between various strata of potentiality, and presented them to contemporary philosophers in a witty and vivid idiom. Thus a reader of Ryle today finds Aquinas much less mysterious than did philosophers of earlier generations.

More recently still a change in philosophical fashion has removed an obstacle to the appreciation of Aquinas's writings on moral philosophy. A generation ago philosophers insisted on a sharp distinction between morals and ethics. Morality concerned first-order questions of right and wrong which affect decisions about what we should or should not do: Is adultery always wrong? Should I be a conscientious objector? Ethics was a second-order discipline which concerned the logic of moral discourse: What logical relations, if any, are there between statements of fact and statements of value and obligation? What are the logical characteristics specific to moral judgements? When ethics alone is regarded as the legimate purview of the moral philosopher, a writer like Aquinas, who makes no sharp distinction between ethics and morals, is likely to be given short shrift. But in very recent years philosophers have become almost as interested in substantive moral questions as their medieval predecessors, and even some of those most prominent in promoting the original distinction between ethics and morals are to be found writing on first-order topics, such as the morality of abortion and the justification of lying, with the same enthusiasm with which Aquinas wrote on the wickedness of usury and the conditions for a just war.

In spite of these recent changes, only a small minority of professional philosophers take much interest in Aquinas. The insights of Wittgenstein have been surprisingly little absorbed by the philosophical community. Interest in logical formalisms which obliterate the distinctions between the potential and the actual ('possible worlds') is currently more fashionable than the serious philosophical study of potentiality. There has indeed been a revival of interest in medieval philosophy among philosophers of a historical bent: but it has concentrated on the areas of logic, linguistics and scientific methodology, in which Aquinas's contribution was slight, rather than on those of metaphysics, ethics and philosophy of mind, in which his most rewarding work is to be found.

Probably the principal reason why Aquinas is not read is the simple and obvious one that his works are written in medieval Latin. Even those who have acquired a good knowledge of Latin at school find it difficult to read scholastic Latin until they become acclimatised; and Aquinas's style is so technical and so economical that it is difficult to produce a clear translation without lapsing into tendentious paraphrase. But a reader once familiar with scholastic convention finds Aquinas's prose smooth and pleasant, and vastly more lucid than that of other medieval philosophers such as Scotus and Ockham. Scholastic Latin even at its most teasing is no more difficult to translate than the greater part of Aristotle's Greek. The study of Aristotle's *Ethics* continues with unabated enthusiasm in a now largely Greekless philosophical environment; there is no reason why the Second Part, which is one of the most fascinating commentaries ever written on that work, should not be studied beside it with equal seriousness.

In the present chapter I have tried to present the main episodes in Aquinas's life, and the main topics of his writings. I have said something of his influence on later thought and his relevance to contemporary philosophy. My discussion has been of necessity extremely sketchy and impressionistic. In the remaining chapters I shall adopt a different method. I shall shift from comprehensive skimming to selective grappling. I shall take two facets of Aquinas's philosophy – his metaphysics and his philosophy of mind – and treat them in sufficient detail to permit the quotation and discussion of individual texts from his writings. In the second chapter I will discuss the metaphysical concepts – matter, form, substance, accident, essence, existence – which permeate Aquinas's writings, and I shall argue that, while his system incorporates valuable insights and important distinctions, that part of it which has often inspired most admiration – his theory of Being

– involves philosophical confusions which not even the most sympathetic treatment can eradicate. In the final chapter I will turn to his philosophy of mind, his account of the human intellect and will and cognitive and affective powers. Here, by contrast, I will argue that in spite of confusions in detail and lacunae of which later philosophers have made us aware, we can find a philosophical structure which is fundamentally sounder than its more familiar rivals, and on which future philosophers will do well to build.

2 Being

Any reader on first opening Aquinas's work finds himself faced with a battery of technical terms which express a number of pervading and difficult ideas. These ideas, according to Aquinas's admirers, combine into an all-embracing system which provides a uniquely favourable framework for the consideration of philosophical problems, and indeed for the consideration of scientific problems of any kind. Such a framework of concepts, transcending the interests of particular scientific disciplines and offering an understanding of the universe at a very general and abstract level, is what is meant when philosophers talk of a *metaphysical system*. It is as a metaphysician, perhaps, that Aquinas is most widely admired.

In the present chapter I will try to expound briefly the main concepts of Aquinas's metaphysics. The concepts which we shall be examining are not, in the main, of Aquinas's own creation: they were inherited from a tradition going back to Aristotle, and they were handed on to other teachers in the schools and universities of the Middle Ages. They form, it may be said, the common patrimony of *scholasticism*, as the philosophy of these schoolmen is called.

These general systematic concepts need to be examined by anyone who hopes to understand anything of Aquinas, since they are to be found in operation on any page of his writing. But their importance, in my view, does not consist in their constituting, in their totality, a coherent system of philosophy. On the contrary, I think that their use by Aquinas often involves ambiguity and confusion. I do not question the judgement that he was a great metaphysician: but I think that his metaphysical insights were often gained in spite of, rather than because of, the apparatus of scholastic concepts which he employed. I will try, in this chapter, to expound the concepts in such a way as to make clear both the overall systematic role which they are supposed to play, and the particular types of confusion and obscurity to which they may lead.

I shall illustrate my account by discussing some of the more important texts Aquinas wrote on the topic. The texts are not easy to understand, and the reader should not expect to comprehend them at first reading. I shall try to explain the main points they contain in language more intelligible to people unfamiliar with scholastic jargon, so that the reader can then return to the texts with enhanced understanding. The process, though difficult, will, I hope, convince the reader that there can be no simple and uncontroversial translation of Aquinas's ideas into terms and concepts immediately intelligible to the contemporary reader.

The English language contains many common words of everyday significance which began life as technical terms of Aristotelian scholasticism: words such a 'accident', 'intention', 'matter', 'substance', 'form', 'quality', 'category', 'property'. The ordinary current meaning of these words is usually somewhat different from their original Aristotelian meaning: an explanation of the latter may serve as an introduction to the metaphysics employed in Aquinas's writings.

The notions of *substance* and *accident* are best introduced by considering, as Aristotle did in his *Categories*, the different types of predicate which may occur in subject–predicate sentences. The theory of categories may be looked on as an attempt to classify predicates. The predicate of a sentence may tell you what kind of thing something is, or how big it is, or what it is like, or where it is, or what it is doing, and so on. We may say, for instance, of Thomas Aquinas that he was a man, that he was enormously large, that he was an intelligent man, that he was younger than Albert the Great, that he lived in Paris, that he lived in the time of St Louis of France, that he sat down when he lectured, that he wore his head shaven, that he wrote many books, and that he was kidnapped by his family. The predicates that we use in saying these things belong – Aristotle would say – in different *categories*: they belong, respectively, to the categories of substance, quantity, quality, relation, place, time, posture, vesture, action and passion. A predication in the category of *substance* tells you, concerning the thing which the sentence is about, which kind of thing it is: a human being, a dog, a chestnut, a lump of gold. That is one meaning of the word 'substance': it can be used to mark off a type of predication, by contrast to predications in the other nine categories, which may be called predications of *accidents*. More importantly, the word 'substance' can be used to refer to the thing that sentences such as the above are about: the object for which the subject-term of the sentences stands. Thus Thomas Aquinas was himself a substance, of whom substantial and accidental predications could be made. The important difference between the two types of predication is this: when a substantial predication ceases to be true of a substance, then that substance ceases to exist; when an accidental predication ceases to be true, then the substance merely changes. Thus Aquinas could cease to live in Paris without ceasing to be Aquinas; but he could not cease to be a human being without ceasing to exist.

Though the relationship between substance and accidents is best explained by reference to subject–predicate sentences, neither substances nor accidents are linguistic entities, or bits of language. The sentence 'Socrates is wise' contains the word 'Socrates', but it is about the man Socrates; and it is the man Socrates, not the word, that is a substance. (Confusingly, both the man and the word may be, in English and in Aquinas's terminology, called 'the subject' of the sentence.) Accidents, likewise, are to be distinguished from accidental predicates: when 'Socrates is wise' is true, what makes the predicate true of the subject is the fact that among the items there are in the world is the wisdom of Socrates; it is this extra-linguistic item, not the predicate of the sentence, that is the accident (M V.1.9 885ff.).

The wisdom of Socrates is not, of course, a substantial entity like Socrates himself: nor is his colour, nor his size, nor his posture. But belief in the reality of accidents does not involve conceiving them as concrete entities like substances, even of the most shadowy kind. The point of the distinction between substance and accident is precisely to draw attention to the way in which Socrates' wisdom is a very different kettle of fish from Socrates. But many of those who believe in accidents – including Aquinas – do invite confusion when they speak of accidents as being parts or constituents of the substance to which they belong. The colour of a tree is not a part of the tree in the way in which its bark and branches and leaves are; and perhaps no one would even be tempted to think that Socrates' being taller than Simmias was a part of Socrates. It is therefore confusing to speak of substance and accidents entering into some sort of composition with each other (as e.g. in S I 3 7). But the confusion to which it may lead – of thinking of accidents as a sort of outer skin or veneer and of substance as an interior kernel or marrow – is one against which Aquinas himself warns from time to time.

One is tempted to draw the contrast between substances and accidents by saying that the former are concrete and the latter abstract. But this is misleading. If by 'concrete' one means 'tangible' then there are substances, such as air, which are not in any simple sense tangible. Moreover, if Aquinas is right, there are substances such as God and the angels which are not tangible in any sense. And on the other hand there are some accidents, such as the roughness of a piece of sandpaper, which are tangible in the straightforward sense of being detectable by the sense of touch. Other accidents are perceptible by other forms of sense-perception: colour by sight, sweetness by taste, and so on. Some are perceptible by more than one sense: shape, for example, is detectable by appearance or by feel. Substances themselves, indeed, are perceptible only by perceiving their accidents: it is because I can see its colour, size, and shape, and because I can hear its miaow and feel its furriness, that I can perceive the cat. This does not mean that substances are imperceptible, mysterious, invisible and intangible entities behind the familiar visible and tangible accidents. But it does mean that tangibility is not the distinguishing characteristic of substance.

That something is a substance of a certain kind, according to Aquinas, is something which only intellect, not sense-perception, can discover; the presence of accidents may be detected by the unaided use of one of the five senses. This seems to be correct. I do not see *what kind of a thing* something is simply by looking, any more than I see *what a thing tastes like* simply by using my eyes. For all that, substances may be perceived. With my eyes I can see, say, sulphuric acid; though it is not just by looking, but by intelligent use of hypothesis and experiment and information that I know that the stuff I see is sulphuric acid.

Is the concreteness of substance and the abstractness of accidents to be sought then in this: that substances are entities with a history which enter into causal relations with each other, while accidents are somehow timeless and insulated from the hurly-burly of the world? No: 'Wisdom', with a capital 'W', may be fancied to exist in some ethereal realm beyond space and time; but the wisdom of Socrates grew through time, had effects in his own life and the lives of others, and was much missed when, with Socrates himself, it disappeared from the world.

Aquinas himself uses, to mark the difference between substance and accidents, two slogans of Aristotelian inspiration, neither of them easy to translate. One is 'accidentis esse est inesse', which means 'For an accident to be is to be of'; the other is 'accidens non est ens sed entis', which means 'An accident is not what is but is of what is'. Both these arcane dicta make the same point: any accident, such as a shape, a smile or a weight, must be an accident *of* something: the shape of something, somebody's smile, some object's weight. There cannot be a shape which is not anything's shape, a smile which is nobody's smile, a weight which is not the weight of any object. Moreover, when we talk of the existence or history of accidents, we are really talking of the modifications and charges of substances: as, when we say that Socrates' cold is worse, we mean that Socrates is sneezing more frequently, having more difficulty breathing, and so on.

Aquinas insists that when God created the world, he created substances, not accidents (S I 45 4c). He warns against the errors of people who think of accidents as shadowy substances (C 11). We may summarise his doctrine as follows: The existence of A's F-ness is nothing other than A's being F; and the coming into being of A's F-ness is nothing other than A's becoming F.

Though Aquinas insists strongly on this point, there are surprisingly many other passages in his writings where he is quite prepared to contemplate the possibility of accidents existing without inhering in any substance. Indeed, he believed that in the sacrament of the Eucharist this actually occurred. After the consecration of the bread and wine, the accidents of bread and wine, he believed, remained in existence after the bread and wine had become the body and blood of Christ. Of course, Aquinas believed that this was the result of the miraculous exercise of divine omnipotence; but he also believed, and often insisted, that even an omnipotent God could not bring about a state of affairs that was self-contradictory.

Some may see in Aquinas's teaching on transubstantiation a simple lapse from the standards of philosophical rigour which he attained when not under the pressure of dogma. But before concluding that this is the explanation, we may inquire whether it is indeed self-contradictory to speak of accidents which are not accidents of any substance. The idea of the Cheshire cat's grin without the cat seems the very quintessence of absurdity. On the other hand, there is nothing miraculous or even mysterious in the smell or taste of onions hanging round after the onions have been eaten. Again, the shape of my boot may remain imprinted in the snow after the boot itself, imprudently placed too near the fire to dry, has gone up in flames. In these cases the accidents are accidents of individual substances now defunct: but the colours of the rainbow, and the blueness of the sky, are colours not attributable to any substance present or past. Are these cases counterexamples to the Aristotelian theses enunciated above?

The truth of the matter seems to be that in Aquinas's writings one finds two quite different notions of *accident*. On the one hand, there is the very general, abstract notion derived from the grammatical consideration of Aristotle's categories: wherever there is a true predication of the form 'A is F', there is an accident describable by a noun-phrase constructed from the predicate (a 'nominalisation' of the predicate): A's F-ness, or A's being F (see opposite). On the other hand, there is a second notion derived from reflection on the ordinary usage of words such as 'shape', 'colour', 'taste', 'smell', 'position' and so on. These words can be used to classify the nominalisations which arise from the Aristotelian schema: since the earth is round, there is such a thing as the roundness of the earth, and this is an instance of a shape. But a very brief reflection convinces one that the ordinary usage of words of this kind extends very much further than the Aristotelian pattern: the 'of' that occurs in expressions such as 'the shape of ...' 'the smell of ...' covers many other relationships besides that of an accident's inherence in a currently existing substance: it may, for instance, be like the 'of' in 'the effect of the explosion' or like the 'of' in 'the story of King Arthur'.

When Aquinas wrote about accidents in the context of transubstantiation, it is clear that it was the popular notion of accident that he had in mind. Thus, facing the problem how accidents without substance can nourish and inebriate, he considers the suggestion that it is the smell of wine that inebriates, as the smell of wine in a full cellar may make a man feel dizzy before he opens a cask. He rejects the suggestion, not on the grounds that an accident is something quite different from a smell, but on the grounds that you can get far more drunk on consecrated wine than you can by going into a cellar and sniffing. (S III 77 6).

If we take the Aristotelian notion of accidents, there is clearly an incoherence in the notion of an accident inhering in no substance: there cannot be any such thing as A's being F if there is no such thing as A. But the popular notion, since it allows a variety of relationships to be indicated by the 'of' in 'the F-ness of A', can allow for the F-ness to exist after the demise of A. Aquinas would have done a service to both his theological and his philosophical readers if, in his writing on transubstantiation, he had distinguished between the two concepts of accident and not spoken as if he was continuing to use the Aristotelian one (as e.g. in S III 77 1 ad 3).

According to the Aristotelian notion, then, an accident is always an accident of a substance and any statement about an accident must be replaceable by one with a substance as a subject. Why, we may ask, cannot the same point be made about substances themselves? If any statement about Socrates' whiteness is reducible to a statement about Socrates being white, cannot we say with equal force that any statement about Socrates must be reducible to a statement about some underlying entity – matter, say, or energy – being in a Socratified form? To answer this question, we must turn from the distinction between substance and accidental form, to the distinction between matter and substantial form. It is substantial form which, in Aquinas, is form *par excellence*.

These concepts of *matter* and *form* have their primary role in Aquinas's analysis of the changes undergone by individual substances. If I have a lump of dough and mould it in my fingers so that it has the appearance first of a boat and then of a woman, it is natural to say that here the same bit of stuff is taking on different shapes. The Latin words 'materia' and 'forma', and still more the Greek words from which they were translated, can have this everyday meaning of 'stuff' and 'shape'. But the moulding of a piece of dough, though it is the kind of thing which Aquinas, following Aristotle, often uses as an illustration to introduce the notions of matters and form, is not strictly a case of a single body of matter taking on two different substantial forms. For a change of shape is an accidental change, not a substantial change: there is here no change from one kind of thing to another kind of thing, no variation of predicates in the category of substance. Moreover, a lump of dough, for Aquinas, is not strictly speaking a substance at all, but rather an artificial conglomerate of a number of natural substances. For there to be a genuine substantial change it is necessary, though not sufficient, that at the beginning of the change there should be a substance of one kind, and at the end of the change there should be a substance of another. Thus the death and decomposition of a dog's body is, for Aquinas, an instance of a substantial change. Here, as in most cases, we do not have a simple case of a single substance of one kind turning into a single substance of another, but a case of a single substance turning into many independent substances, the various natural elements into which the body decomposes. This is a one–many substantial change; when I eat and digest a varied meal we have the inverse case of many–one substantial change.

For there to be a genuine substantial change it is not sufficient that there should be an episode which starts with substance A and ends with substance B. For such an episode to be a change as opposed to, say, a miraculous replacement of one substance by another, it is necessary that there should be something in common between the substance present at the beginning of the change and the substance present at the end of the change. One way of explaining the concept of *matter* is to say that matter is what is common to the two termini of a substantial change. When substance A, which is of kind F, turns into substance B, which is of kind G, then there is some stuff which is the same parcel of stuff throughout the change and which prior to the change is F-ish and at the end of the change G-ish.

This, at least, is the explanation suggested by several passages in Aquinas. For instance:

In every change there must be a subject of change which is first in potentiality and then in actuality . . . The form of that into which something is turned begins to exist afresh in the matter of that which is turned into it; thus, when air is turned into fire which does not previously exist, the form of fire begins to exist afresh in the matter of the air; and similarly, if food is turned into a previously non-existent human being, then the form of a human being begins to exist in the matter of the food. (S III 74 4 1 2 and ad 1 2)

Aquinas's first example of a substantial change shows that in his
mind analysis into matter and form was bound up with a primi-
tive scientific theory according to which the elements of the
bodies of our world were earth, air, fire and water. Composite
bodies are made up of these four elements, and can be decomposed into them: but a change from one of these elements
into another is not a decomposition into anything simpler, for
there is nothing simpler. We might quite naturally regard the
elements themselves as the matter out of which composite bodies
are made: if I pull up a handful of celery from the vegetable
patch and eat it all up, we might say that all the bits of earth and
water which were once informed by the form of a plant are now
informed by my human form. They could indeed exist separately
simply as bits of earth and bits of water. But earth and water and
fire and air are not themselves made out of any bits which can
exist separately. Yet, on Aquinas's theory, they can change into
each other, so there must be something common to them all,
something which they are all made of. This he calls *prime*
matter. Thus:

The pre-existent matter into which compound bodies can be decomposed is the four elements: but there cannot be any decomposition
into prime matter, which would result in its existing without any form,
because matter cannot exist without form. (S III 75 3)

How far can the concepts of matter and substantial form be
detached from the archaic physics with which they are associ-
ated? The medievals' earth, water and air seem to be the ancestors
of our notions of solid, liquid, and gas: and these seem to be
states of matter rather than constituents of substances. (Not until
the development of plasma physics did fire have a chance of
returning to parity with the other three elements.) In so far as
chemists recognise substantial changes – changes from one
chemical substance into another – a change from water into
steam is something which does *not* count as a substantial change.

However, though the analysis of chemical change is something
immensely more complicated than Aquinas allows for, this fact
itself does not invalidate the notion of prime matter. This notion
was supposed to have application precisely at the point at which
chemical analysis ceased, wherever that may be. It is not in cases
where we can say such things as 'This H_2O was first ice, and is

now water' or 'This hydrogen was first combined with oxygen and is now combined with sulphur' that the concept of prime matter applies: it is in cases where there is no description such as 'H_2O' or 'hydrogen' which applies to the stuff all the time before and after the change that Aquinas will speak of what is common to the termini of the change as being *prime* matter. It seems doubtful whether there are any such cases: at every level appropriate descriptions seem to be available until we come to the point at which the identification of matter itself becomes problematic, as in subatomic physics. A recent writer, Peter Geach, has well said:

To say there is *no* room for the conception of *the same matter* or *the same stuff* in modern science would indeed be wrong; a scientist might very well investigate whether, and how fast, an apparently unchanging body was in fact undergoing an interchange of matter with the environment; or again he might want to know which parts of a man's body were nourished by a given substance, and perhaps use radioactive 'tracers' to show where the ingested stuff went. But the application of such talk to fundamental physics seems out of the question; the identification of parcels of matter seems here to lose its sense, and so indeed does the idea of a perfectly unleaky vessel.

It is most commonly with regard to the life-cycle of living beings that Aquinas and his followers make use of the notion of prime matter and substantial form. Aquinas held that in a living creature there was only a single substantial form at a given time. Even though an animal can do many of the same things as a plant (e.g. self-nourishment and propagation) this does not mean that it has one form in common with plants which makes it a living thing, and another form in addition which makes it an animal. It has a single specific form which enables it to perform all of its characteristic vital functions at every level. It follows from this that when I pluck and eat the celery it is not strictly true to say – as we suggested above – that there are some bits of water which were first part of the celery and are later parts of me: for there are no bits of matter which first had the form of celery and later had the form of humanity, *and throughout had the form of water.* The form of water is merely 'virtually contained' in the form of celery in the sense that whatever a bit of matter could do in virtue of being water it can also do in virtue of being part of an organic whole which has the form appropriate to celery.

It is not easy to know by what arguments, or even by the practice of what discipline, we are to settle the question how many substantial forms there are in, say, a living dog. Hence, it is hard to know whether to agree or disagree with Aquinas that there is only a single substantial from in each substance. But it is correct to say that *if* a substance can have only one substantial form at a time, then the matter of which the substance is composed must be prime matter in the sense of being matter which at that time has no other from.

Prime matter is sometimes represented as a mysterious, incomprehensible and barren entity, or perhaps rather a non-entity: it is defined as something of which nothing can be truly predicated, since predication would involve the attribution of form to what is of its nature essentially formless. But there is a confusion and an ambiguity in describing matter as formless. Do we mean matter united to no form, or matter having no form?

In one sense, formless matter would be matter which is united to no form. In this sense, Aquinas is emphatic that there is no such thing as formless matter: matter without form cannot exist even by divine power. Discussing the doctrine of some Church Fathers that matter was first created unformed, he says:

If unformed matter means matter lacking all form whatever, then it is impossible to say that a period of formlessness preceded the formation and variegation of matter. This is obvious in the case of formation: for if formless matter was prior in time then it already existed in actuality ... but form and actuality are the very same thing; hence to say that matter pre-existed without form is to say that something actually existed without actuality, which involves a contradiction. (S I 66 1)

In another sense, however, matter *can* be said to be formless. For strictly speaking matter does not *have* forms. Its relation to form is not that of *having*. What *has* the form is the substance, the matter-form composite. Matter is a kind of potentiality: when air is turned into flame, this shows that the air had the potentiality of turning into flame. The matter which is common to air and flame is precisely their capacity to turn into each other. But the potentiality of being flame is not what has the form of air: it is the air that has the form of air, and the air that has the potentiality too.

On the one hand, then, matter cannot exist except in union

with some form or other, and on the other hand, matter can remain the same matter while parting from any given form you may mention. It is because of this that substantial change differs from accidental change and that substantial forms are distinct from accidental forms. When a substance loses one accidental form and gains another – when a chameleon changes colour, for instance – there is always a form, the substantial form (of chameleonhood), which it possesses throughout the change. But when a parcel of matter is first a human being and then a corpse, there is no form to which the matter is united throughout the change.

Thus, Aquinas says of matter:

Matter receives form: and by receiving form it possesses existence as an instance of a particular kind of thing, air or fire or whatever it may be. (S I 50 2 ad 2)

Matter is actually existent only by form. Whatever is made up of matter and form ceases from actual existence through the separation of the form from the matter. (S I 50 5)

One could not similarly say that a substance was actually existent only by having accidents. Of course, substances such as human beings must have a multiplicity of accidents – they must have some shape or other, some size or other, some colour or other and so on – but it is not in virtue of these accidents that substances exist and are what they are. A substance could lose any particular accident without ceasing to be what it is but if it lost its substantial form it *would* cease to exist.

In considering Aquinas's theory of accidents we found side by side in his writings an abstract philosophical notion and a more concrete popular one. The same is true of the theory of matter. Sometimes matter is introduced simply as the potentiality for substantial change: to say that something is material is simply to say that it is capable of changing into a substance of a different kind. Sometimes matter is thought of as that which *has* the capacity to change: whether this be the substance itself (as one might say of a human being that he was, among other things, a chunk of matter), or a part of the substance (as when we are told that when we say 'air has the potentiality of being flame' we are strictly talking about only that part of the air of which, when the flame has come to be, it will be true to say that it *is* the flame (S III 75 8)).

Many things can be said about matter in the popular sense which would be nonsense to say about it in the philosophical sense. One could not say of a thing's potentiality to change that it had been cut into two pieces, or that it had a certain size: it is only matter as what *has* the potentiality that can be said to have dimensions. This is important because it is matter as characterised by dimension that Aquinas says is what philosophers call the 'principle of individuation' in material things. He means that, for instance, two peas, however alike, however many accidental forms they may have in common in addition to their substantial form, are two peas and not one pea because they are two different parcels of matter. It seems that if we wish to avoid confusion in thinking about matter it is best to take it, not as potentiality, nor as a part of a substance, but as a substance *qua* capable of change.

If we understand matter in this way, we can explain substantial form, correspondingly, as what makes a bit of matter to be a substance of a particular kind. (The kind may be natural or artificial: Aquinas is prepared to allow that an artefact such as bread is a substance (S III 75 6 ad 1).) When we say that form makes matter substance, the word 'makes' must not be misunderstood: we are using it in the sense in which we might say that it is the Great Pyramid's shape which makes it a pyramid – we are not talking about one thing acting causally on another from outside, as when we say that rain makes the grass grow. Aquinas's favourite expression for a form is 'that by which, or in virtue of which, a thing is what it is' (*id quo aliquid est*). A substantial form is that in virtue of which a thing is the kind of thing it is; that, indeed, in virtue of which it exists at all. An accidental form is that in virtue of which something is F, where 'F' is some predicate in one of the categories of accidents.

The substantial forms of material objects are individual forms. Peter, Paul and John may share the same substantial form in the sense that they each have the substantial form of humanity; but if we are counting forms, the humanity of Peter, the humanity of Paul, and the humanity of John add up to three forms, not one. What makes Peter, Paul and John three men and not a single man is their matter, and not their form; but the matter, in individuating the substances, also individuates their substantial forms. Aquinas would have regarded as unacceptable the Platonic notion that Peter, Paul and John are all men by sharing in a single common form of Humanity (S I 50 2).

Aquinas and his followers sometimes talk as if in a sentence such as 'Peter is a man' or 'Socrates is wise' we could explain the meaning of the predicates by saying that each of them referred to a form – a substantial form in the first example and an accidental form in the second example. This can hardly be correct. In the first place it is clear that 'Peter has the substantial form of humanity' is intelligible to us only because we are told that it is equivalent to 'Peter is a man': the notion of form is explained in terms of the meaning of predicates, and not the other way round. In the second place, the theory fails to account for the meaning of false sentences. It seems clear that all the words in a sentence must stand for the same thing whether the sentence is true or false. If a question admits of the answer 'Yes' or 'No', the reference of all the words in the question must be the same no matter what the answer may be. But if the sentence 'Socrates is wise' is false, there is no such thing as the wisdom of Socrates for the sentence to be about.

When Aquinas says that material bodies are composed of matter and form, or that matter and form are parts of bodies, he does not mean that matter and form are elements out of which bodies are built, or pieces into which they can be decomposed. Matter, as we have seen, is incapable of existence without form; and forms, unlike bodies, are not made out of anything. Many of the things which Aquinas says about forms seems to imply that they cannot exist without matter any more than matter can exist without form. If forms do not themselves exist, but are only that in virtue of which substances exist, it seems clear that there cannot be a substantial form which is not the form of any substance. And this, indeed, Aquinas seems to have accepted.

Surprisingly, however, Aquinas thought that in addition to material substances, composed of matter and form, there were also immaterial substances which consisted of pure form. It was thus that he conceived the angels of Judaeo-Christian tradition, which he identified with the cosmic intelligences postulated in Greek and Arabic astronomy. Now there is nothing inconceivable in the notion of a substance, which is not material in the sense of being generated out of, or corruptible into, material substances of other kinds. Such a substance might even be intelligent: an imperishable crystalline oracle, capable of motion but not of substantial change, would be in that sense an immaterial intelligence. The idea seems fanciful, but not inconceivable Aquinas believed that the visible heavenly bodies were immaterial in this limited sense: they were made out of a fifth element or 'quintessence' which had no potentiality for taking on any other substantial form and was capable only of changing its whereabouts. But the angels he held to be immaterial in the stronger sense of being pure form.

True to his doctrine that if two things have similar substantial forms it is their matter which individuates them, Aquinas maintained that there could not be more than a single immaterial angel of any given kind. Peter and Paul belonged to the same species, being different parcels of matter with similar human forms; Michael and Gabriel were each unique members of differing species, as different from each other as a human being is from a fish (S I 50 4).

Aquinas's speculations on angels are often fascinating for the sidelong light which they throw on his philosophical theories about more mundane entities: but his doctrine of pure forms seems to be a lapse into the Platonism against which he was continuously anxious to guard in his account of material substances. I do not mean to pronounce on the conceivability of the notion of immaterial intelligence; I mean merely that if the idea of an immaterial substance can be made coherent it is better presented not as an instance of pure form but as an instance of a type of substance to which the doctrine of matter and form does not apply. But even with regard to material substances, Aquinas is prepared to allow an exception to his general thesis that the substantial forms of material objects exist only in the existence of the substances whose forms they are. The exception is allowed in the case of the souls of human beings.

Aquinas regarded the souls of human beings, and indeed of all living things, as particular instances of substantial forms. As an Aristotelian he considered that animals and vegetables had souls no less than human beings: a soul was simply the principle of life in organic living beings, and there are many non-human organisms. The special privilege of human beings was not their possession of a soul, but their possession of a rational or intellectual soul. Now human beings grow and take nourishment, just as vegetables do; they see and taste and run and sleep just as animals do. Does this mean that they have a vegetable and animal soul as well as a human soul?

Many of Aquinas's contemporaries answered this question in the affirmative. They held that in the human being there was not just a single form, the intellectual soul, but also animal and vegetable souls; and for good measure some of them added a further form, a form which made a human being a bodily being. This was a 'form of corporeality' which human beings had in common with stocks and stones just as they had a sensitive soul in common with animals and a vegetative soul in common with plants.

Aquinas rejected this proliferation of substantial forms. He maintained that in a human being there was only a single substantial form: the rational soul. It was that soul which controlled the animal and vegetable functions of human beings, and it was that soul which made a human body the kind of body it was: there was no substantial form of corporeality making a human body bodily. If there had been a plurality of forms, he argued, one could not say that it was one and the same human being who thought, loved, felt, heard, ate, drank, slept and had a certain weight and size. When a human being died there was a substantial change; and, as in any substantial change, there was nothing in common to the two terms of the change other than prime matter.

These opinions of Aquinas aroused opposition among his theological colleagues, and among the propositions condemned at Oxford in 1277 were the two following:

The vegetative, sensitive and intellectual souls are a single noncomposite form.

A dead body and a living body are not bodies in the same sense.

The theological opposition to Aquinas was based on doctrinal premises. For instance, it was argued, if there was nothing other than prime matter in common between the body of Christ when alive and his body when placed in the tomb, then the body in the tomb was not the same body as the living body of Christ; and it was therefore not a fit object of worship as Christian tradition had maintained.

In time the theologians gave up their objections and Aquinas's rejection of the plurality of forms became the common theological opinion. But there are serious philosophical difficulties in the identification of soul with form; or, to put the point in another way, it is not clear that the Aristotelian notion of 'form', even if coherent in itself, can be used to render intelligible the notion of 'soul' as used by Aquinas and other Christian philosophers.

The first problem is this. If we identify the human soul with the Aristotelian substantial form, it is natural to identify the human body with Aristotelian prime matter. But body and soul are not at all the same pair of items as matter and form. This is a point on which Aquinas himself insists: the human soul is related to the human body not as form to matter but as form to subject (S I–II 50 1). A human being is not something that *has* a body; it *is* a body, a living body of a particular kind. The dead body of a human being is not a human body any longer – nor indeed any other kind of body, but rather, as it decomposes, an amalgam of many bodies. Human bodies, like any other material objects, are composed of matter and form; and it is the form of the human *body*, not the form of the matter of the human body, that is the human soul.

Secondly, and more seriously, just as we found side by side in Aquinas a philosophical and a popular notion of *accident* and of *matter*, so the notion of *form* seems in his writings to be doing double duty. The form of humanity is introduced as being, truistically, that by which a man is a man, or that which makes a man a man: the 'makes' being, as explained, the 'makes' of formal casuality, as when we say that it is a certain shape which makes a piece of metal a key, or a certain structure which makes a molecule a DNA molecule. But Aquinas often speaks of the soul as being causally responsible – through its powers, the intellect and the will – for the various activities which make up a human life. And here the causality is efficient causality, the sort of causality for which nowadays the word 'cause' is commonly reserved, as when we are told that it is the yeast that causes the bread to rise or that DNA molecules cause the synthesis of proteins. It is this kind of relationship that is suggested when we are told that the soul is the principle of life. The two motions of form seem to be different from each other and impossible to combine, without confusion, into a single notion.

Thirdly, Aquinas believed that the human soul was immortal and could survive the death of the body, to be reunited with it at a final resurrection. Hence, by identifying the soul with the human substantial form he was committed to believing that the form of a material object could continue to exist when that object had ceased to be. Consistently with his view that a human being was a particular type of body, he denied that a disembodied soul was a human being; but he insisted that it remained an identifiable individual and this in turn led him into a series of inconsistencies. He had to insist that a human soul was individuated although there was no matter to individuate it, despite the fact that matter, on his own theory, is what individuates form. He maintained that individual disembodied souls continued to think and will after the demise of the human beings whose souls they are, in spite of his own frequent insistence that when there is human thought and volition it is not the intellect or the will, but the human being that does the thinking and willing (e.g. G II 73). If the substantial form of Peter is what makes Peter a human being, how can it continue to exist when the human being Peter is dead and gone? A human being's being human is surely something that ceases when the human being ceases.

The doctrine of the survival of the substantial form clashes with the most important of Aquinas's theses about form: that which links form and *esse* or existence. To *be* simply is to continue in possession of a certain form: *omnis res habet esse per formam.*

It is to Aquinas's doctrine of *esse* that we must now turn. 'Esse', the Latin verb 'to be', has most of the uses of its English counterpart, and other uses in addition. It can be used as a copula, linking subject-term to predicate-term in a sentence, as in the English sentences 'Socrates is wise', 'You are a fool.' It can be used to indicate existence, as the English verb can in such sentences as 'There is a plant in Brazil which devours insects' or 'Caesar is no more.' The Latin verb can be used as the grammatical predicate to indicate the existence of what corresponds to the subject term, as in 'Deus est', 'There is a God.' The equivalent use in English is rare and archaic.

Existence itself, as the two examples above illustrate, can be attributed in various ways. When we use 'exists' in a way cor-

responding to the English 'There is a . . .' construction, we are
saying that there is something in reality corresponding to a certain description, or instantiating a certain concept: thus, when
we say 'King Arthur never existed' or 'God exists' we mean that
no one in reality ever answered to the descriptions which story-
tellers have given us of King Arthur; or that there is in reality,
and not just in fiction or imagination or make-believe, an entity
with the attributes of divinity. We might call this 'specific existence': it is the existence of something corresponding to a certain
specification, something exemplifying a species, for instance,
such as the insect-eating plant. But when we say 'Julius Caesar is
no more' we are not talking about a species, we are talking about a
historic individual, and saying that he is no longer alive, no
longer among the things that live, move, and have their being in
the world. We might call this 'individual existence'.

The Latin verb 'esse' can be used to indicate either kind of
existence: thus 'Deus non est', literally 'God is not', could be used
to assert either that there is no such thing as God (God is and
always has been a mere fiction) or that God is no more – that
God is dead in the quite literal sense that the creator of the world
has passed away (a hypothesis sometimes entertained by philosophers as an explanation of why the world is in such a sorry
state).

Aquinas often draws distinctions between different senses of
'esse'. He distinguishes, for instance, between 'esse' as a copula
and the 'esse' of individual existence. Here are two passages typical of many:

'Esse' is used in two ways . . . In one sense it signifies the actuality of
being (*actus essendi*). In the other sense it signifies the mental attach-
ing of a predicate to a subject which constitutes a proposition. (S I 3 4
ad 2)

'Esse' is used in two ways . . . In one sense it is a verbal copula sig-
nifying the putting together of any kind of sentence which the mind
constructs: this *esse* is not anything in the nature of things, but only in
the mind forming affirmative and negative propositions. In this sense
esse is attributed to anything about which a proposition can be formed,
whether it is a being or only a lack of being: for we say that there *is*
blindness. In another sense it is the actuality of a being in so far as it is
being (*actus entis in quantum est ens*). (Q 9 3)

The verb 'to be' as a copula occurs in sentences such as 'Socrates is wise.' In such a sentence it may be said to 'signify' – in the sense of 'express' or 'effect' – the putting together of the subject 'Socrates' and the predicate 'wise' in the thought of the sentence. (That it 'signifies' in this way does not mean that it signifies anything in the sense of referring to or denoting anything in the way that 'Socrates' does.) Not all sentences which are of subject-predicate form contain the verb 'to be' in this way: e.g. 'Churchill smokes.' But Aquinas, following Aristotle, maintains that every such sentence contains an implicit copula which can be made explicit, as in 'Churchill is a smoker' (M V.8 889). Modern logicians, rather than assimilate subject-verb sentences to subject-copula-predicate sentences, regiment logically in the other direction, and treat not 'white' but 'is white' as the predicate of 'Socrates is white.' More accurately, they treat the predicate as being '. . . is white': i.e. what is left of the sentence if you remove the subject-name from it.

It is puzzling when Aquinas, in the second passage quoted above, gives 'There is blindness' as an example of an attribution of *esse* in the copula sense, since the sentence does not seem to be a subject-predicate one at all. He seems to be stating a general principle that wherever you can construct a proposition of the form 'S is P' you can assert 'P-ness is' or 'There is P-ness.' Does he mean that a proposition of the form 'P-ness is' is equivalent to 'Propositions can be formed with "P" as predicate' or that it is equivalent to the proposition 'Something is P'? It is clear from other passages that it is the second reading he has in mind. Thus:

Esse sometimes signifies the truth of a proposition, even in the case of things which do not have *esse*, as we say that there is blindness, because it is true that (a) man is blind. (P 7 2)

Clearly it is the *truth* of propositions of the form 'S is P', not the mere possibility of forming them, that is in question. 'There is blindness' would no longer be true if the World Health Organization brought it about that no one was any longer blind; though it would still, of course, be possible to form propositions of the form 'X is blind' – in that fortunate state of affairs, false propositions.

Wherever we have a true proposition, then, of the form 'S is P' we can say 'There is P-ness.' But not everything which *is* in this sense *is* in the contrasted sense which 'signifies the actuality of being'. Blindness is not something positive, an ability like sight-edness; it is the lack of an ability. For Aquinas only positive realities, not negative ones, have being or *esse* in the non-copula sense. 'The actuality of being' means individual existence as we earlier explained the term.

Not only substances but also accidents may have individual existence: it is not because blindness is not a substance that it does not have the actuality of being, but because it is a negative attri-bute rather than a positive one. Thus we are told:

Being in this sense is attributed only to things which fall under the ten categories; and thus Being named from this sort of existence is divided into ten kinds. But this sort of being is attributed to things in two different ways.

In one way it is attributed to that which strictly and truly has *esse*, or *is*: and in this way it is attributed only to a self-subsistent substance . . .

But all those things which are not self-subsistent, but exist in and with something else, whether they are accidents or substantial forms or any sort of parts, do not have being in such a way that they really *are* themselves, but being is attributed to them in a different way; that is to say, they are things *by* which things *are*; just as whiteness is said to *be*, not because it is self-subsistent, but because by it something else is white (*habet esse album*). (Q 9 3)

In passages such as the above the translator finds himself forced to use the archaic 'is' as a predicate standing on its own, as in the cases italicised. Moreover, the English word 'being' has now had to do duty, in different contexts, for three different Latin words: the infinitive 'esse' ('to be' or 'being' used as a verbal noun, as in the case of the first word of the passage just quoted); the medi-eval Latin gerund 'essendum' (with a similar sense, but providing a more perspicuous construction in contexts such as the 'act of being', 'actus essendi'); and the participle 'ens', another medieval coinage, meaning 'that which is or exists', as 'the living' means 'those that live.'

Philosophers and logicians who have considered existence in the present century have concentrated on specific existence, and for the sake of logical perspicuity they have preferred to cast statements of specific existence in the 'There is a . . .' form. Thus any sentence of the form 'Fs exist' is rewritten for logical pur-poses. 'There is at least one *x* such that *x* is F' or more simply 'Something is F.' One reason why logicians prefer this form is that it makes it easier to make sense of negative existential propositions such as 'Extra-terrestrial intelligences don't exist.' If we take this as a straightforward subject–predicate sentence we seem to get into a muddle: for if it is true there doesn't seem to be anything in the universe for the subject 'extra-terrestrial intelligences' to refer to, and it is obscure *what* it is that we are predicating non-existence of. (We cannot say that we are predicating non-existence of the ideas in fanciful people's minds: the fancies exist all right, whether or not the extra-terrestrial intelligences do.) Whereas if we say 'There is no x such that x is an extra-terrestrial intelligence' or 'Nothing in the universe is an extra-terrestrial intelligence' that problem disappears.

Contemporary philosophers often quote the slogan 'Existence is not a predicate.' This means that statements of specific existence are not to be regarded as predications about any individual. Statements of individual existence, on the other hand, such as 'The tomb of St Peter still exists' are genuinely about what their subject-term stands for.

We are now in a position to consider Aquinas's most celebrated doctrine concerning *esse*: the thesis that in all created things essence and existence are distinct, whereas in God essence and existence are to be identified. This doctrine can be understood in several different ways, since there is more than one way of understanding 'essence', and since 'existence' may mean specific or individual existence.

In the youthful *De Ente et Essentia* Aquinas introduced the distinction in the following way. Every essence can be thought of without anything being known about its actual existence; for I can understand what a man is, or what a phoenix is, without knowing whether these things exist in reality (*esse habeant in rerum natura*): what a thing is is different from whether there is such a thing, its *quidditas* differs from its *esse*. Here it is clear that it is specific existence that is in question: in modern terminology, Aquinas is saying that one may grasp the concept of phoenix without knowing whether the concept is instantiated. And what is meant by the quiddity of a phoenix is clearly simply the meaning of the word 'phoenix'; as there aren't any phoenixes there cannot be any question of any scientific investigation of the nature of phoenixes. So understood, the doctrine of the distinction between essence and existence seems perfectly correct;

but so understood the doctrine that God's essence is identical with his existence is manifest nonsense. It would mean that to know that God exists is the same as to know what the word 'God' means, and that in answer to the question 'What does "God" mean?' one could sensibly answer 'There is one.'

In other works, Aquinas makes clear that when he is talking about existence he means the individual existence of a given creature, and that by the essence of a given creature he means something as individual as its individualised form. Thus, the existence of a particular dog Fido is something which begins when Fido comes into the world and which ends with Fido's death; the essence of Fido is something which is very bit as individual as Fido's soul is.

Thus, in arguing in the *Summa Theologiae* that in God essence and existence are not distinct, Aquinas says that any existence which is distinct from the corresponding essence must be an existence which is caused by something external to the thing whose existence it is. It is, he argues, because we cannot say that God has an external cause that we must say that in him essence and existence are not distinct (S I 3 4). In passages such as this it is clear that the essence of, say, a dog is not simply the meaning of the word 'dog': it would be absurd to speak of the meaning of a word 'F' as exercising an influence on the existence of Fs which could be compared to the causal efficacy whereby a dog's parents bring the dog into existence. But it is not in the same way absurd to think of a soul as something within an animal which has a causal efficacy in promoting its continued existence. We may be able to make some sense of this idea: but if we can, even so it is quite clear that the soul of a dog is something quite different from the meaning of the word 'dog'.

If we take essence and existence in this way, there is no longer anything clearly absurd about the doctrine that in God essence and existence are not distinct. But what are we to make of the distinction between existence and essence in creatures? Can we say that Fido's essence and Fido's existence are distinct?

Clearly we cannot do so if we mean that one could have the one without the other. For a dog to exist is simply for it to go on being a dog, and for a human being to continue to exist is for it to go on possessing its human nature or essence. Peter's continuing to exist is the very same thing as Peter's continuing to possess his essence; if he ceases to exist he ceases to be a human being, and vice versa.

Some philosophers have believed that there are individualised essences of non-existent beings; that long before Adam and Eve were created there already were such things as the essence of Adam and the essence of Eve; and that the creation of Adam and Eve consisted precisely in God giving existence to these essences, actualising these potentialities. To someone who thinks in this way, the relation of existence to essence will appear exactly parallel to that of form to matter or accident to substance: all three will be in the same way instances of actualisations of a potentiality. But Aquinas, though his language sometimes suggests such a fancy, is customarily quite clear that creation does not involve the actualisation of any pre-existent potentiality. He believed, surely rightly, that just as there cannot be any actualisation without individuation (whatever exists in the world is individual, not universal), so there can be no individuation without actualisation (only what actually exists can be identified, individuated, counted). Is not the real distinction between essence and existence therefore unintelligible, or at best vacuous?

One way to try to make sense of the doctrine is to recall that Aquinas thought it conceivable, though false, that the world might have existed for ever. Had it existed for ever, it would still have been created and still, from all eternity, have owed its existence to God. Similarly, though there is never a time when the essence of Peter is one of the things that there are and Peter does not exist, it remains true throughout the time of Peter's existence that he might never have existed, had God so wished. To say that his essence is distinct from his existence would then be to say that there is nothing about what he is from which it could be concluded that he had to exist. There is no necessity about his existence; it is, as philosophers say, a *contingent* matter. It cannot be proved by any 'ontological argument' based simply on the meaning of words.

Again, one might argue for a distinction between essence and existence in creatures in the following way. While it is true that any creature's existence persists for exactly the same length of time as its essence, there is this difference, that its existence at one time does not have consequences for its existence at a later time in the way that its essence at one time may have consequences for its existence at a later time. A human being tends to go on living for a certain time; a radioactive element tends to go out of existence at a certain rate. These tendencies may reasonably be said to be part of the essence of these creatures: they are tendencies to continue to exist or to cease to exist because of the kind of thing they are. Their essences, therefore, may be said, in a misleading but intelligible way, to *make* them go on existing or cease to exist as the case may be. Essence, therefore, would be distinct from existence as cause is distinct from effect.

This, I think, is the best that can be done to make the doctrine intelligible. However charitably interpreted, the distinction between essence and existence seems an unfortunate way to present a radical difference between God and creatures. For if we do not believe in pre-existent potentialities of creatures, their essence and existence are equally contingent. Moreover, one could not know anything about the essence of a particular creature without thereby knowing that that creature existed. And again, according to Aquinas, even in the case of God, where essence and existence are identical, any ontological argument is equally invalid. And if creaturely essences can be regarded as causes of creatures' transitory existence, why cannot the divine essence be looked on as the cause of God's everlasting existence? God has lived and will live for ever, because of the kind of thing he is.

The doctrine of the identity of essence and existence in God is itself ambiguous. Sometimes Aquinas presents the thesis as meaning simply that the distinction between essence and existence which we draw in the case of creatures is inapplicable to God, since he is a being devoid of any kind of complexity or composition, including the compounding of essence with existence. In conformity with this way of presenting the doctrine, Aquinas frequently says that we do not and cannot know the essence of God – though of course we know what the word 'God' means, otherwise we could not talk about God at all (e.g. S I 2 2 ad 3) (see below, p. 66).

But in other passages Aquinas presents the doctrine that God's essence is his existence as if it meant that we *do* know the answer to the question 'What is God's essence?': the answer being *esse*. Thus, in the *De Potentia* he offers the following proof that in God *esse* and nature or essence are the same. Wherever causes whose special effects are diverse produce also a common effect, the common effect must be produced in virtue of some superior cause of which it is the special effect. For example, pepper and ginger, besides producing their own proper effects have it in common that they produce heat; they do this in virtue of the causality of fire, of which heat is the proper effect.

All created causes, however, have a common effect which is *esse*, in spite of having distinct characteristic effects. Heat makes things *to be* hot, a builder makes there *to be* a house. They have it in common, then, that they cause being; they differ in that fire causes heat whereas the builder causes a house. There must, therefore, be a supreme cause in virtue of which they all cause things to be, and of this cause *esse* will be the characteristic effect. This characteristic effect, however, of an agent proceeds from it as a likeness of its nature; it follows, therefore, that *esse* itself is the substance or nature of God. (P 7 2c)

Two things are clear from this passage. One is that Aquinas is not simply saying that the distinction between existence and essence has no application in the case of God because the very terms are inappropriate or incongruous. He is saying that God's essence is *to be* in the same way as the essence of fire is *to be hot*. Secondly, this being is a very common attribute; or, perhaps we should say, this be-ing is a very common activity. It is an attribute which is possessed, or an activity which is performed, by anything which is anything, that is to say, by anything which possesses any accidental or substantial form, by anything of which any true predications can be made. 'Esse', so understood, seems to be either a predicate variable (to say that x is, in this sense, is to say that for some F, x is F, i.e. that there is some predicate true of x) or else a disjunction of predicates (to say that x is, in this sense, is to say that x is either F or G or H . . . and so on through the list of predicates). Such a predicate, we might say, seems to be the totally uninformative highest (but minimal) common factor of all predicates: but being, so understood, would be too thin and universal an attribute to be the essence of anything. There seems, moreover, a special difficulty in the notion of *pure* being, if being is understood in this sense.

The difficulty is well brought out by an objection which Aquinas himself makes to the proposal that in God essence and existence are the same (S I 3 4 objection 1):

If this is the case, then God's *esse* has nothing added to it. But *esse* without any addition to it is the common *esse* which is predicable of all things; it follows then that God is being in the sense in which being is predicable of everything. But this is false, according to the Book of Wisdom, 14, where it is complained that 'they gave the incommunicable name to stocks and stones'. So God's *esse* is not his essence.

The common *esse* seems to be *esse* as described in the *De Potentia* passage, which really does belong to fire and houses, and therefore presumably to stocks and stones as well. Here, in the *Summa*, Aquinas says that it is not this *esse* that is the essence of God. '*Esse* without addition', he says, may mean '*esse* which specifies nothing further' or '*esse* which permits no further specification'. Common *esse* is *esse* which specifies nothing further: if told simply that Flora *is*, I am not told whether she is a girl or a goddess or a cyclone, though she may be any of these. But God's *esse* is *esse* which permits no further specification. Other things are men or dogs or clouds, but God is not anything, he just is (S I 3 4 ad 1).

But if the 'esse' which denotes God's essence is like the 'esse' which is predicable of everything, except that it does not permit the addition of further predicates, then it is a predicate which is totally unintelligible. For it is tantamount to a predicate variable for which no predicate is substitutable, or a disjunction of predicates which is true of an object though none of the disjoined predicates are true of it. If this is what is meant by saying that God is pure being, then the doctrine is nothing but confusion.

Someone may protest that it is incorrect to take the relationship of 'being' to 'being a house' as that of variable to substitution, or disjunction to disjunct. Perhaps St Thomas means that a house, during its existence, is doing *two* things: (*a*) being a house, and (*b*) just being. Here 'being' would not be as it were an unspecific description of what it is doing in being a house, but rather a description of something else which it is doing in addition. But the only sense which we seem to be able to attach to this 'being' is that of being among the things that there are, being present in the universe of existents. But to say that God was pure being in that sense would be, as we saw before, to say that God's essence consisted in there being such a thing as God, which again is nonsense (see above, p. 54).

The most promising clue which Aquinas offers to enable us to make sense of his doctrine of essence and existence is his frequent

use of the Aristotelian dictum 'vita viventibus est esse': 'for living
things, to be is to live'. Let us try, then, to make sense of 'esse' by
comparing it with 'live'. My life consists of many activities: I
walk, I eat, I sleep, I think. While I do these things I am alive;
but living is not some other activity which I am performing while
doing these things, as breathing is; they are themselves parts of
my life, it is in doing them that I am living. 'Live' is not a
disjunction of these activities, as '... is an animal' could be
regarded as a disjunctive predicate equivalent to ' ... is a human,
or a cat, or ...'. We can see this if we reflect that being asleep, for
instance, is part of living, whereas being a human is not part of
being an animal; rather the other way round. Aquinas gives a
precisely similar reason why the predicate 'ens', 'being', does not
denote a genus whose species would be particular types of being.
(S I 3 6). Just as my life is not an accompaniment, or component,
or highest common factor of all the various things I do during it,
but rather the totality of them all, so the *esse* of anything is not
something underlying, or constituting, or specifying its characteristic and modifications; it is rather the totality of all the episodes and states of its history. It seems to be in this sense that
Aquinas can speak of *esse* as 'the actualisation of all acts, and the
perfection of all perfections' (P 7 2 ad 9).

If we take *esse* in this way, we can see how Aquinas can deny
that *esse* is the most indeterminate and empty predicate, and why
he insists that it is in fact the richest and fullest predicate and
therefore the most appropriate to capture the divine perfection
(S I 4 1). But our earlier problem returns in a new form. When
Aquinas says that God is *pure* being, or subsistent being, he
means that nothing more can be said about God's essence other
than that God *is*; and this not because of our ignorance, but
because of the pure and undiluted form in which being is present
in God. But if we take 'esse' in the sense of 'life' or 'history', then
the notion of pure being is as empty as the notion of pure life or
pure history. There could not be a life which consisted of
nothing but just living, or a history uncontaminated by anything
actually happening. The attractiveness of this way of taking 'esse'
was that it allowed us to conceive it as a rich totality rather than
as an impoverished common factor. But if 'esse' is taken thus,
then pure esse is a totality which has no parts, and its 'richness' is
its entire lack of any property.

The theory of the real distinction between essence and existence, and the thesis that God is self-subsistent being, are often presented as the most profound and original contributions made by Aquinas to philosophy. If the argument of the last few pages has been correct, even the most sympathetic treatment of these doctrines cannot wholly succeed in acquitting them of the charge of sophistry and illusion.

3 Mind

One of the motives which have led men through the ages to the study of philosophy has been the desire to understand their own nature. In particular, men have turned to philosophy to seek a greater insight into the nature of their own minds. From ancient times philosophers have tried to gain this insight by reflection on their own mental processes and abilities, and by consideration of the language which we use to express and describe our mental states. In recent centuries there have grown up a number of scientific disciplines devoted to the study of mind – branches of experimental, social and clinical psychology. The information acquired by these disciplines assists us enormously in the understanding of human nature: but they do not compete with, and cannot supersede, the philosophical study of the mind. This is because the relationship between the phenomena studied by the scientist and the mental events or states which are manifested in these phenomena is itself a philosophical problem: it is the central problem of the philosophy of psychology, or what is nowadays commonly called 'philosophy of mind'. Because of the enduring nature of the philosophical framework for the study of mind, the writings of ancient, medieval, and seventeenth- and eighteenth-century philosophers of mind have not been antiquated by the progress of science, as their writings in some other areas have. In particular, I shall argue, the writings of Aquinas on the topics nowadays treated by philosophers of mind remain of value.

According to Aquinas, human beings, unlike animals, have a capacity which he calls the 'intellect' or 'understanding' (*intellectus*). The Latin word 'intellectus' is connected with the verb 'intelligere': this is commonly translated 'understand' but in Aquinas's Latin it is a verb of very general use corresponding roughly to our word 'think'.

We employ the word 'think' in two quite different ways: we talk of thinking *about* something, and we talk of thinking *that* something. Thus, in the first way, we may say that someone abroad thought of home, or thought of his family; in the second way we may say that someone thought that there was a prowler downstairs, or that there was likely to be an increase in the rate of inflation. In one usage, but not in the other, the verb introduces an *oratio obliqua* or indirect speech construction. We might, if we wished, call thoughts reported in these two different ways two different kinds of thought: thinking *of*, and thinking *that*. This would be a little misleading, because thinking *that* involves thinking *of* (you cannot think that inflation will increase without thinking of inflation), and because thinking *of* X is usually thinking *that* X something-or-other (as thinking of the family may take the form of thinking that the family will just now be sitting down to breakfast). So it is probably preferable to make the distinction as a linguistic one between two uses of 'think' rather than between two types of thought.

Aquinas, however, makes the corresponding distinction in Latin as a distinction between two different acts of the intellect: he speaks of the *intelligentia indivisibilium* (literally 'the understanding of things that are not complex') on the one hand, and *compositio et divisio* (literally 'putting together and taking apart') on the other. Here is a typical passage:

There are, as Aristotle says in the *De anima*, two kinds of activity of our intellect. One consists in forming simple essences of things, such as what a man is or what an animal is: in this activity, considered in itself, neither truth nor falsehood is to be found any more than in non-complex utterances. The other consists in putting together and taking apart, by affirming and denying: in this truth and falsehood is to be found just as in the complex utterance which is its expression. (V 14 1)

In what way is 'putting together' contrasted with what is 'non-complex'? Is it simply that after the verb 'intelligere' when it means 'think of' there follows a single word, whereas when it means 'think that' there follows a combination of words into a clause? No: the matter is more complicated than that, as Aquinas makes clear. The clearest instance of what Aquinas calls 'compositio et divisio' is the making of affirmative and negative judgements. Now whether I judge that the cat is on the mat, or that the cat is not on the mat, the words 'cat' and 'mat' are put together in the sentences that express my judgement. But in the affirmative judgement I as it were in thought put the cat and the mat together, and in the negative judgement I in thought put them apart – which does not, of course, mean that I put the *thought of* the cat apart from the *thought of* the mat. Thus Aquinas explains:

> If we consider the state of affairs in the intellect on its own, there is always putting together wherever there is truth and falsehood; these are never to be found in the intellect unless the intellect puts one non-complex thought next to another. But if thoughts are considered in their relation to reality, they are sometimes called *compositio* and sometimes *divisio*. They are called *compositio* when the mind puts one idea next to another as a way of grasping the putting together or identity of the things they are ideas of: they are called *divisio* when the mind puts one idea next to another as a way of grasping that the things are diverse. This is how it comes to be that an affirmative sentence is called a *compositio* (signifying a conjunction in reality) and a negation is called a *divisio* (signifying a separation in reality). (H 1 3 26)

Thus we have the following schema:

$$\left\{ \begin{array}{l} \text{Understanding of non-complex (expressed in single words)} \\ \text{Complex} \quad \left\{ \begin{array}{l} \text{compositio (expressed in affirmative} \\ \text{\quad sentences)} \\ \text{divisio (expressed in negative sentences)} \end{array} \right. \\ \text{understanding} \end{array} \right.$$

It is the first distinction in this schema, rather than the distinction between positive and negative judgements, that is the important one; and this distinction between two types of intellectual act, between two types of thought, is indeed connected with the difference between the use of individual words and the construction of sentences. Any act of thought, Aquinas explains, can be regarded as the production of an inner word or utterance.

> The 'word' of our intellect ... is that which is the terminus of our intellectual operation: it is the thought itself, which is called an intellectual conception; which may be either a conception which can be expressed by a non-complex utterance, as when the intellect forms the essences of things, or a conception expressible by a complex utterance, as when the intellect makes affirmative or negative judgements (*componit et dividit*). (V 4 2c)

When I have the thought that *p*, the content of the thought has the same complexity as the sentence which would give it expression if I expressed the thought. (This is not to be regarded as a remarkable parallelism discoverable by armchair psychology: it is simply that we have no criteria for the simplicity or complexity of thoughts other than the criteria for the simplicity or complexity of the words and sentences that give them utterance.)

Not all thoughts are given public expression in words, of course: I may say to myself, behind clenched teeth, 'What a frightful bore this man is!', while being deterred by politeness from letting such a thought show. Some thoughts are not even put into words in the privacy of the imagination: the wanderer's thought of his family at breakfast may be simply an image of them sitting in the kitchen, not the internal enunciation of any proposition. But whenever I judge that something is the case there is always a form of words that would express the content of my judgement: that is guaranteed by the indirect speech construction, since the *that*-clause, suitably modified, will provide the necessary form of words.

A thought may have the complexity expressible by a complete sentence without being a *judgement* to the effect that something is the case: instead of positively thinking that the cat is on the mat I may merely wonder whether the cat is on the mat or simply entertain the idea of the cat on the mat as part of a story or fantasy. Any thought which has the complexity of a sentence may be a true thought – a thought that is in accord with the facts – without being *judged* to be true. In many cases, the thought that *p* is just as thinkable as the thought that not-*p*, as Aquinas observes (V 14 a2c), and what makes a man opt for one or other side of a contradiction, if he does, will differ in different cases. Judgement may be withheld because of lack of evidence on either side, or because of the apparent equality of the reasons pro and con; judgement may rest on the self-evident truth of a proposition, or be the result of a more or less prolonged train of reasoning; judgement may be tentative and hesitant, or firm and unquestioning. Aquinas classifies exercises of the intellectual powers on the basis of these different possibilities: the withholding of judgement is doubt (*dubitatio*); tentative assent, allowing for the possibility of error, is opinion (*opinio*); unquestioning assent to a truth on the basis of self-evidence is understanding (*intellectus*); giving a truth unquestioning assent on the basis of reasons is knowledge (*scientia*); unquestioning assent where there are no compelling reasons is belief or faith (*credere, fides*). Forming a belief, accepting an opinion, entertaining a doubt, coming to a conclusion, and seeing a self-evident truth are all instances of the second type of intellectual activity: *compositio et divisio*.

What of the other intellectual activity: *intelligentia indivisibilium*? I introduced Aquinas's distinction by comparison with the distinction in English between *thinking of* and *thinking that*. And this English distinction, which we have laboured to make more precise, does indeed correspond to the distinction which Aquinas is making between simple and complex objects of thought. But Aquinas seems to have another distinction in mind at the same time. Besides contrasting *thinking of* and *thinking that*, we can contrast *knowing about* and *knowing that*, and the passage I quoted earlier from the *De Veritate* suggests that the first type of activity is instantiated not so much by, say, thinking of a hawk but rather by knowing what a hawk is. But thinking of a hawk and knowing what a hawk is are not two rival activities at the same level. Thinking of a hawk is an exercise of the ability which constitutes knowing what a hawk is: for knowing what a hawk is is precisely the ability to do such things as talk about hawks, think about hawks, tell them from handsaws and the like. The distinction between the two is, in scholastic terms, a distinction not so much between two activities as between two degrees of actuality. It is like that between having the ability to recognise a particular Greek letter and actually using that ability to read off a word; the former, scholastics said, is a first actuality and the latter a second actuality. The same distinction between degrees of actuality can be drawn in the case of the second activity of the intellect: knowing that the Battle of Waterloo took place in 1815 is an actuality – it is not the same as the mere potentiality, the mere ability to learn the fact, that is possessed by a schoolboy just beginning history – but it is only a first actuality, an actuality that is potentiality by comparison with actually calling to mind and consciously making use of that knowledge. So instead of the dichotomy which St Thomas suggests, there is really a fourfold division:

	Intelligentia indivisibilium	*Compositio et divisio*
First actuality	Knowing what X is	Knowing (believing etc.) that *p*
Second actuality	Thinking of X	Thinking (calling to mind etc.) that *p*

First actualities are dispositions rather than occurrences: they are, as Aquinas would say, *habitus*, matters of having knowledge rather than exercising it; they are states a human being is in rather than activities upon which he is engaged. The second actualities which are the exercises of first actualities are, by contrast, datable items in a person's history, activities which are more or less clockable, capable of being interrupted or repeated, and so on.

Knowing what X is is something which itself can take two forms. There is the everyday knowledge of what a hawk is which anyone has who knows what the word 'hawk' means: sometimes Aquinas is willing to call this knowledge of the meaning of a word knowledge of what a thing is, or knowledge of its 'quiddity', from the Latin word 'quid', which means 'what' (e.g. E 5). But commonly he distinguishes between the knowledge of what the word 'X' means and knowledge of the quiddity or essence of X. Thus, for instance, he often says that we know what the word 'God' means but that we cannot know the essence of God (S I 3 4 ad 2 and 48 2 ad 2). Knowledge of essence seems to be some kind of scientific knowledge of the nature of a thing: but it is not clear in Aquinas's writings whether knowledge of the essence of a hawk would be the kind of thing which might nowadays be found in the writings of ornithologists, or whether it is the kind of knowledge, beyond their most optimistic dreams, which would give the power to synthesise or create an artificial surrogate of the bird. Certainly Aquinas says from time to time that the essences of things are unknown to us: but it is not clear whether he means this as a statement about the human condition or a lament about the state of contemporary science.

Aquinas, as I began this chapter by saying, regards the intellect as a capacity which is not shared by animals other than human beings. How can this be so, if the intellect is the capacity for thought? Surely a dog, when he sees his master take the lead off the hook on the wall, thinks that he is going to be taken for a walk and expresses the thought in a very clear manner by leaping and bounding about and pawing at the door. No doubt there are certain thoughts – about history, poetry or mathematics, for instance – which are beyond the capacity of dumb animals; but it surely cannot be claimed that the capacity for thought itself is peculiar to human beings.

Aquinas does in fact allow to animals the ability to think

certain types of thought. Obviously, many animals share with human beings the capacity for sense-perception; but as they also look for things which are not currently within the range of their perception they also have some notion of what is absent. They can discriminate between, and derive pleasure or pain from, sensory properties; but this does not exhaust their discriminatory power.

If the only things that moved an animal were things pleasurable and repugnant to the senses, there would be no need to suppose any power in it except the perception of sense forms in which it would either take pleasure or displeasure. But an animal has to seek and shun things not only because they suit or do not suit its senses but also because they are in other ways fitting and useful or harmful. Thus a lamb, when it sees a wolf approach, flees, not because it does not like the colour or shape, but because it is its natural enemy. And likewise a bird collects straw, not because it pleases its senses, but because it needs it for building its nest. So the animal has to perceive things which no external sense perceives. (S I 78 4)

The power of grasping ideas which are not simply sense ideas is called 'a power of estimation' (*vis aestimativa*); since Aquinas thought that such ideas were all inborn in animals, while being acquired by human beings through association, the *vis aestimativa* can not unfairly be called in English 'instinct'. In addition to an instinctive grasp of what is useful and dangerous Aquinas attributes to animals a memory for such properties. He even attributes to them a concept of pastness as such, which many philosophers would find difficulty in attributing to a non-language-user. But he sees a difference between human memory and animal memory in that while both humans and animals remember things, only humans can try to remember things or make efforts to call things to mind: in his terminology animals have *memoria* but not *reminiscentia*.

The most obvious and the most profound difference between human beings and, say, sheep, fish and birds is the possession of language. If we want 'intellect' to mean a characteristically human capacity then it seems most helpful to regard the intellect as the capacity for thinking those thoughts that only a language-user can think. (Thoughts that only a language-user can think are thoughts for which no expression in non-linguistic behaviour can be conceived: e.g. the thought that truth is beauty, or that there are stars many light-years away.) Would Aquinas agree with this characterisation of the intellect?

It is difficult to be sure. On the one hand, Aquinas attributes intellect to God and to angels who are not, in his view, language-users like human beings, even if on occasion they use human language to communicate with mankind. On the other hand, Aquinas often implicitly, and sometimes explicitly, describes the working of the intellect as a linguistic operation. Thus, for instance, in comparing the intellect with the senses he has this to say:

Two types of activity occur in the sensory part of the soul. One is simply a modification (*immutatio*): operation of the sense-faculty is brought to completion by the modification effected by the perceptible object. The other is a creative activity, whereby the imagination forms for itself an image (*idolum*) of something absent, or something perhaps never seen.

In the intellect these two types of activity are combined. First there can be observed the modification of the receptive intellect when it is informed by an intellectual idea. Thus informed, it proceeds to form a definition, or a negative or affirmative proposition expressed by an utterance. A concept expressible by a name is a definition; a sentence is what expresses the *compositio* and *divisio* of the intellect. (S I 85 ad 3)

Here intellectual activity is contrasted with the play of mental imagery precisely as being the creation of the mental counterparts of the words and sentences of public language.

Aquinas says that the human intellect understands, or thinks of, things by abstracting from 'phantasms' (*phantasmata*). By 'phantasms', for the moment, we can take him to mean sensory experience, including the images of things absent and never seen which were spoken of in the passage quoted above. Intellectual activity, then, is regarded as in some way dependent on sense-experience; in some sense of the word Aquinas is an empiricist. Many empiricist philosophers have held that all our ideas arise from sense-experience, and that they are acquired by abstraction from or selective inattention to features of that experience. But Aquinas differed from the empiricists most familiar to British readers in that he assigned to the intellect a very much more active and complicated role in the activity of abstraction.

Indeed, for Aquinas, the intellect was not one faculty but two, or rather a single faculty with two powers: the agent intellect (*intellectus agens*) and the receptive intellect (*intellectus possibilis*). It was the agent intellect which was the human capacity to abstract universal ideas from particular sense-experience; it was the receptive intellect which was the storehouse of those ideas once abstracted.

Aquinas postulated an agent intellect because he thought that the material objects of the world we lived in were not, in themselves, fit objects for intellectual understanding. A Platonic idea, universal, intangible, unchanging, unique, existing in a noetic heaven, might well be a suitable object for intellectual understanding; but then there are not, according to Aquinas's official theory, any such things as Platonic ideas. In a sense, Aquinas maintained, the intellect can understand only things that are its own creation.

Plato thought that the forms of natural things existed apart without matter and were therefore thinkable: because what makes something actually thinkable is its being non-material. These he called *species* or ideas. Corporeal matter, he thought, takes the forms it does by sharing in these, so that individuals by this sharing belong in their natural kinds and types; and it is by sharing in them that our understanding takes the forms it does of knowledge of the different kinds and types.

But Aristotle did not think that the forms of natural things existed independently of matter, and forms existing in matter are not actually thinkable. Nothing passes from potentiality to actuality except by something already actual, as sense-perception is actuated by something which is actually perceptible. So it was necessary to postulate a power belonging to the intellect to make actually thinkable objects by abstracting ideas (*species*) from their material conditions. That is why we need to postulate an agent intellect. (S I 79 3)

The word *species* which is transliterated in the above passage is a word which plays a very important role in Aquinas's theory of thought. It appears first as a synonym for the Platonic word 'idea', but it is used also for the actually thinkable objects which figure in the Aristotelian theory. The English word 'idea' is indeed the best to capture the multiple facets of the sense of the Latin word *species*, and I shall hitherto use it in preference to the transliteration.

The most intelligible part of the difficult passage just quoted is the comparison between sense and intellect, which Aquinas goes on to develop in the answers to objections in the same article. Colours are perceptible by the sense of sight: but in the dark, colours are only potentially, not actually perceptible. The sense of vision is only actuated – a man only sees the colours – when light is present to render them actually perceptible. Similarly, Aquinas is saying, the things in the physical world are, in themselves, only potentially thinkable or intelligible. An animal with the same senses as ours perceives and deals with the same material objects as we do: but he cannot have intellectual thoughts about them – he cannot, for instance, have a scientific understanding of their nature – for the lack of the light cast by the agent intellect. We, because we can abstract ideas from the material conditions of the natural world, are able not just to perceive but to think about and understand the world.

Does this mean that Aquinas is an idealist? Does he believe that we never really know or understand the world itself, but only immaterial and abstract ideas?

The answer to this question is complicated. In Aquinas's system there seems to be descriptions of two quite different types of ideas: ideas that are mental abilities, and ideas that are mental objects.

Sometimes we read of ideas that are dispositions or modifications of the intellect. Ideas of things in this sense seem to be what would nowadays be called 'concepts': you have a concept of X, for instance, if you have mastered the use of a word for X in some language. Ideas may be ideas *that*, instead of being ideas *of*: an idea *that* such and such is the case would be an instance of an idea corresponding to Aquinas's second type of acts of the intellect, just as an idea *of* something corresponds to the first type of act. An idea *that*, considered as a disposition, would be a belief or opinion or something of the kind, rather than a simple concept. In this sense, then, ideas are dispositions corresponding to the two types of thought which are the activities by which the intellect is defined.

If a philosopher thinks of ideas in this way, he is unlikely, one might expect, to be tempted to think of ideas as the *objects* of our understanding, as *what* we know when we have knowledge. If I am thinking about the North Pole, no doubt I am making use of, employing, or exercising my concept of the North Pole; but my concept is not what I am thinking *about*. If I think that the

North Pole is a cold sort of place, or that it was discovered by Peary, I am not thinking that my concept is cold or was discovered by Peary, but that the Pole itself is/was. Of course I *can* think about my concept of the North Pole: I can reflect, for instance, that it is a rather thin, hazy and childish one; but in thinking that thought in turn I am not thinking that the North Pole is thin, hazy and childish; and I am exercising not merely my concept of the North Pole but also my concept of *concept*. When we take ideas in this sense, then, it may be true to say that all thought uses ideas, but it is obviously untrue to say that all thought is about ideas.

Aquinas makes this point quite clearly:

Some thinkers have maintained that our cognitive powers are aware only of their own modifications . . . thus the intellect would think of nothing but its own modification, that is the ideas which it takes in. On this view, ideas of this kind are the very object of thought. But this opinion is obviously false . . . If the only objects of thought were ideas in our souls, it would follow that all the sciences are not about things outside the soul but only about ideas in the soul . . . (S I 85 2)

The truth is that ideas are not *what* is thought of (*id quod intelligitur*) but that *by which* thought takes place (*id quo intelligitur*):

But because the intellect reflects on itself, by the same act of reflection it thinks of its own thinking and of the idea by which it thinks. And thus the idea is a secondary object of thought; but the primary object of thought is the thing of which the idea is a likeness. (S I 85 2)

Aquinas, then, explicitly rejects the idealist doctrine that the mind can think of nothing but its own ideas. But there are a number of features of his writing which tempt the reader to think that he regarded ideas not simply as abilities or dispositions to think in certain ways, but as the primary objects of thought. In the passage quoted above, as in many other places, Aquinas speaks of the idea as a likeness of the thing of which it is an idea; and this suggests that ideas are pictures or images from which we read off the features of their originals. If this were right, then external things would be the primary objects of thought only in the sense in which, when I look at myself in the mirror, I 'see' myself rather than seeing the mirror, unless I am making an especial effort to attend to the mirror. But this would be a wrong way to interpret Aquinas: elsewhere he expressly distinguishes between mental images in the imagination (*idola* or *phantasmata*) and the ideas of the intellect; and in explaining what he means by saying that an idea is a likeness of its object, the comparison he introduces is not that of portrait to original, but that of the resemblance between cause and effect in natural processes.

There are two kinds of actions, Aquinas says: those which result in changes in the patient on which the agent acts, and those which affect nothing but the agent. Sometimes he calls actions of the first kind 'transient' and actions of the second kind 'immanent'. When a fire heats a kettle, we have an action of the first kind, and when I think of a kettle, we have an action of the second kind: heating the kettle brings about a change in the kettle, but thinking of the kettle of itself affects nothing but the thinker. What heats the kettle is the heat of the fire: the cause of the heating resembles the object after the change. St Thomas goes on:

Similarly, the form operative in an immanent action is a likeness of the object. Thus, the likeness of a visible thing is operative in the sight of vision, and the likeness of an object of thought, i.e. an idea, is operative in the thinking of the intellect. (S I 85 2)

The parallel seems clumsily drawn: the way in which the ter-minus of an immanent action (a particular thought) resembles the operative form (an idea or concept) is that both of them are *of the same object*: it is their similarity to each other, not to the object *of* which they are, that is parallel to the heating of the kettle.

Is there, then, any sense in which an idea or thought is like its object? Surely nothing could be more different than, say, salt and my being able to recognise salt: indeed 'difference' seems too weak a word to describe the gulf between the two items. But an idea is like its object in this way: in order to identify an idea one has to describe its content; and the description of the content of the idea is the very same as the description of the idea's object. For instance, the idea that the world will shortly come to an end might be said to be the idea of a certain state of affairs: to specify *which* idea is involved, and to specify *which* state of affairs is involved one uses exactly the same expression 'that the world will shortly come to an end'.

Though Aquinas did not accept the thesis that the intellect can know nothing but its own ideas, he rejected also the contrasting thesis that it is possible to grasp material objects by a purely intellectual thought. When I think of a particular human being there will be, if I know him well, very many descriptions I can give in language to identify him. But unless I bring in reference to particular times and places there may be no description I can give which could not in theory be satisfied by a human being other than the one I mean: I cannot individuate the person I mean simply by describing his appearance, his qualities. Only perhaps by pointing, or taking you to see him, or calling to mind an occasion on which we met can I make clear which person I mean: and pointing and vision and this kind of memory are matters of sense, not of pure intellectual thought.

Our intellect cannot have direct and primary knowledge of individual material objects. The reason is that the principle of individuation of material objects is individual matter; and our intellect understands by abstracting ideas from such matter. But what is abstracted from individual matter is universal. So our intellect is not directly capable of knowing anything which is not universal. (S I 86 1)

It is by linking intellectual ideas with sensory experience that we know individuals and are capable of forming singular propositions such as 'Socrates is a man'. Let me explain what this means.

For Aquinas the real object of all human knowledge is form. This is true of sensory acquaintance and intellectual understanding. The senses perceive the accidental forms of objects that are appropriate to each modality: with our eyes we see the colours and shapes of objects, with our noses we perceive their smells; colours, shapes and smells are accidental forms. These forms are individual forms – it is the colour of *this rose* that I see and even the most powerful nose cannot take in the smell of the universal *sulphur*. Substantial form, on the other hand, is something that can be grasped only by intellectual thought (see above, p. 35): the proper object of the human intellect is the nature of material things. Material things are composed of matter and form: the individuality of a parcel of matter is not something that can be grasped by the intellect. The intellect can grasp what makes Socrates a man, but not what makes him Socrates:

Essence or nature includes only what defines the species of a thing:

thus human nature includes only what defines man, or what makes man man, for by 'human nature' we mean that which makes man man. Now the species of a thing is not defined by the matter and properties peculiar to it as an individual; thus we do not define man as that which has this flesh and these bones, or is white, or black, or the like. This flesh and these bones and the properties peculiar to them belong indeed to this man, but not to his nature. An individual man then possesses something which his human nature does not, so that a man and his nature are not altogether the same thing. (S I 3 3)

If Plato was wrong, as Aquinas thought he was, then there is not, outside the mind, any such thing as human nature as such: there is only the human nature of individual human beings such as Tom, Dick and Harry. But because the humanity of individuals is form embedded in matter, it is not something which can, as such, be the object of pure intellectual thought. To conceive the humanity of Tom, Dick or Harry, we need to call in aid the imagination. The humanity of an individual, in Aquinas's terminology, is 'intelligible' (because a form), but not 'actually intelligible' (because existing in matter) (see pp. 69–70 above). That is to say, it is, because a form, a fit object of the understanding; but it needs to undergo a transformation if it is to be actually held in the mind. It is the agent intellect which, on the basis of our experience of individual human beings, creates the intellectual object, humanity as such.

This, then, is the degree of truth in the suggestion that Aquinas was an idealist. The ideas are not intermediate entities which represent the world: they are modifications of the intellect consisting in the acquired ability to think certain thoughts. But the universals which the ideas are ideas *of* are themselves things which have no existence outside the mind.

Aquinas is aware that the charge can be made that on his account the intellect distorts reality in the very process of grasping it. He puts to himself the following objection:

A thought which thinks a thing otherwise than it is is a false thought. But the forms of material things are not abstracted from the particulars represented in experience. Hence, if we think of material things by abstracting ideas from experience, there will be falsehood in our thought. (S I 85 1)

His reply depends upon distinguishing two senses of the ambiguous sentence 'A thought which thinks a thing otherwise than it is,

is a false thought.' To think a thing *to be* otherwise than it is is
certainly to think falsely. But if all that is meant by our 'thinking
a thing otherwise than it is' is that the way it is with our thinking
when we think is different from the way it is with the thing we
are thinking about, in its own existence, then there need be no
falsehood involved. To think that Julius Caesar had no weight
would be to think a false thought; but there is no falsehood
involved in thinking of Julius Caesar without thinking of his
weight. A thought of Julius Caesar can perfectly well exist without a thought of his weight, though Julius Ceasar himself could
not exist without his weight. Similarly, Aquinas argued, there can
be, without any distortion or falsehood, a thought of human
nature which does not contain a thought of any individual
matter, though there never was an instance of human nature
without any individual matter (S I 85 1 ad 1).

The account which Aquinas gives of the operation by which
the agent intellect abstracts ideas from sense-experience is obscure in detail and probably confused; but he is surely right to
insist on attributing to human beings a special abstractive power
unshared by other animals. In order to possess the type of concepts which we use to refer to and describe the objects of our
experience it is not at all sufficient merely to have sensory experience. Children see, hear and smell dogs before they acquire the
concept *dog* and learn that the word 'dog' can be applied to
labradors, poodles and dachshunds but not to cats and sheep;
they feel pricks and aches and cramps long before they acquire
the concept *pain*. The family pets live in much the same sensory
environment as the family baby: the baby, but not the pets, learn
from what is to be seen and heard the mastery of symbols to
describe and change that environment. In its broadest outlines,
the theory of the agent intellect is nothing other than the recog-
nition that concept-formation cannot be simply regarded as the
residue of sense-experience.

Aquinas's theory of the agent intellect places him in a middle
position between empiricist philosophers who regard ideas as
arising from the observation of recurrent features of experience
and rationalist philosophers who claim that individual ideas are
inborn in every member of the species. Aquinas thought that
there were no fully innate ideas or beliefs: even belief in self-
evident propositions he allowed to be innate only in a very

qualified sense. A human being, he maintains, once he knows
what a whole is and what a part is, knows that every whole is
greater than any of its parts; but, he continues, a man cannot
know what a whole is or what a part is except through the possession of concepts or ideas derived from experience (S I–II 51
1). To this extent Aquinas agrees with empiricists against the
rationalists that the mind without experience is a *tabula rasa*, an
empty page. But he agrees with the rationalists against the empiricists that mere experience, of the kind that humans and
animals share, is impotent to write anything on the empty page.

Among contemporary thinkers one who is very close to the
position of Aquinas on this matter is the linguist Noam
Chomsky. Chomsky has argued that it is impossible to explain
the rapidity with which children acquire the grammar of a
language from the finite and fragmentary utterances of their
parents unless we postulate a species-specific innate language-
learning ability. Chomsky himself compares his theory to the
theories of rationalists such as Descartes: but the very general
nature of the faculty he potulates – it has to be extremely general
if it is to explain the learning of all the many diverse natural
languages – does not at all closely resemble the very specific
ideas postulated by the rationalists, which corresponded often to
individual words in language. It is much closer to the general-
ised, species-specific ability to acquire intellectual concepts from
unstructured sense-experience which Aquinas called the agent
intellect.

The agent intellect, then, is the capacity to acquire intellectual
concepts and beliefs. The receptive intellect (*intellectus possibilis*) is the ability to retain and employ the concepts and beliefs
thus acquired.

One and the same soul ... has a power called the agent intellect,
which is a power to make other things actually immaterial by abstracting from the conditions of individual matter, and another power to
receive ideas of this kind, which is called the receptive intellect as
having the power to receive such ideas. (S I 79 4 ad 4)

The receptive intellect is the storehouse of ideas (S I 79 6); it is
the initially blank page on which the agent intellect writes. At
any given moment in a human being's history there will be a
repertoire of intellectual skills he has acquired and a stock of

opinions, beliefs and knowledge which he possesses. That repertoire and that stock make up the contents of his receptive intellect. Sometimes Aquinas's language invites us to think of the receptive intellect as a kind of spiritual stuff which takes on new forms as a thinker acquires new ideas (e.g. S I 79 6). But he warns us against taking this seriously, and puts us on our guard against the dangers of applying the notions of matter and form to the relationship between the intellect and its ideas (e.g. S I 84 3 ad 2). It is because of the Aristotelian comparison that to this day we speak of being *informed* about a matter and call the gaining of knowledge the acquisition of *information*.

The agent intellect and the receptive intellect are two powers which correspond to two uses of the English word 'mind'. When we say that human beings have minds but dumb animals do not, we may mean that humans, but not animals, have the ability to acquire abstract information from sense-experience. When we talk of someone as having a richly stocked mind, it is the contents of his receptive intellect that we are talking about. We also use the word 'mind' and the adjective 'mental' in another way. We contrast doing sums on paper with doing sums in our heads: and we call the latter 'mental arithmetic'. Clearly the agent intellect and the receptive intellect are involved equally in a complicated calculation whether it is done publicly or silently: we must be meaning something else by 'mind' when we regard the silent workings as more 'mental' than the public manipulation of symbols. The mind considered as the locus of mental images and silent monologue is called by Aquinas the imagination or fancy (*phantasia*) and is regarded by him as an interior sense rather than as a department of the intellect.

Sense-perception, according to Aquinas, was, like the acquisition of intellectual information, a matter of the reception of forms in an immaterial manner.

A sensory form exists in one manner in the thing which is outside the soul, and in another manner in the sense itself, which receives the form of sensible objects without their matter – the colour of gold, for instance, without the gold. (S I 84 1)

Forms thus received by the sense were, according to Aquinas, stored in the fancy. They may be reshuffled at will to produce phantasms of anything we care to think about: we can combine, for instance, the form which represents Jerusalem and the form which represents fire to make the phantasm of Jerusalem burning.

Aquinas's account of the relation between sense and imagination is in some respects naïve and unsatisfactory: he calls the imagination an inner sense and his picture of how it operates is modelled far too closely on the operation of the senses. He seems to have thought that an inner sense differed from an outer sense principally in having an organ and an object inside the body instead of outside the body. He does indeed observe that others beside the perceiver may check up on what he claims to see with his senses, while in the case of the 'inner senses' there is no such thing as putting a man right about the contents of his mental image. But – as Aquinas does not seem to realise – this makes it inappropriate to speak of the imagination as a sense. For a sense faculty which cannot go wrong is not a sense-faculty at all.

Unlike some others who have regarded the imagination as an inner sense, however, Aquinas has a clear grasp of the relationship between the intellect and the imagination when thought takes place in mental images or in subvocal speech. In such cases it is not the imagery that gives content to the intellectual thought, but the intellect that gives meaning to the imagery – whether imagined words or mental pictures – by using it in a certain way and in a certain context. When I think of Troy, maybe I conjure up an image; but it is not that image's likeness to Troy which makes it an image of Troy; it is the thoughts with which I surround it and the words in which I would express those thoughts. In the book of our thoughts, it is the intellect that provides the text; the mental images are only illustrations.

On the other hand, Aquinas often states that phantasms are necessary not only for the acquisition of concepts but also for their exercise. In this life at least it is impossible for us to think any thought except by attending to phantasms. We can see this, he says, if we reflect that injury to the brain can impede thought, and if we remember that we all conjure up pictures when we are doing our best to understand something. However dubious these arguments may be, it does seem to be true that there must be some exercise of sense or imagination, some application to a sensory context, if we are able to pin down someone's habitual knowledge or beliefs to their exercise on a particular occasion.

Attention to phantasms, then, is, according to Aquinas, necessary for any thought, even of the most abstract and universal
kind. But a special type of attention called 'reflection' (*reflexio
supra phantasmata*) is needed if the thought is to be a thought
concerning individuals rather than universals. As explained above,
Aquinas thought that only the appropriate accompanying mental
imagery or sensory context would differentiate a thought about
Socrates from a thought about Plato or about any other human
being.

Sense-perception and intellectual thought, as we have said, are
both, for Aquinas, matters of the reception of forms in a more or
less immaterial manner in the mind. In both perception and
thought a form exists, as Aquinas puts it, 'intentionally'. When I
see the redness of the setting sun redness exists intentionally in
my vision; when I think of the roundness of the earth, roundness
exists in my intellect. In each case the form exists without the
matter to which it is joined in reality: the sun itself does not enter
into my eye, not does the earth, with all its mass, move into my
intellect.

Intentional existence is not, however, as such, immaterial
existence. According to Aquinas redness exists intentionally not
only in my eyes, but in the lucid medium through which I see it
(S I 56 a2); and even in the eye the sensible form is a form of the
matter to be found in the sense-organ. But in the intellect there is
no matter for the forms to inform. The receptive intellect indeed
has no other nature than its ability to be informed by forms
existing intentionally: if it had, it would be incapable of understanding whatever shared its nature, as coloured spectacles pre-
vent one from discriminating white light from light of their own
colour (S I 75 2 and 87 1).

The occurrence of concepts and thoughts in the intellect is not
a case of the modification of any matter: there is no moulding of
mysterious mental material.

Each thing is known according to the ways its form exists in the
knower. But the intellective soul knows a thing's nature just so and
absolutely. The form of stone, for instance, just so and absolutely, in
its proper formal meaning, is in the intellective soul. Consequently the
intellective soul is a form just so and absolutely, and not something
composed of matter and form. For were it composed of matter and
form, the forms of things would be received into it in all their concrete

individuality, so that it would know only the singular, as the senses do, which receive forms of things in a physical organ; for materiality is the principle that individuates form. (S I 75 5)

Aquinas's doctrine of the intentional existence of forms remains one of the most interesting contributions ever made to the philosophical problem of the nature of thought. Suppose that I think of a phoenix. There seem to be two things which make this thought the thought it is: first, that it is a thought *of a phoenix*, and not a thought of a cow or a city or an asymptote; secondly, that it is *my* thought and not yours or Julius Caesar's. Other things may be true of thoughts – e.g. that they are interesting, unpleasant, detailed etc. – but these seem to be the two things essential to any thoughts, that they should be *someone's* thoughts, and that they should be thoughts *of something*. Now both these properties of thoughts raise deep philosophical problems.

The question 'What makes my thoughts *my* thoughts?' may not strike one as problematic at all; but many people have been puzzled by the problem of the relation of a thought to what it is a thought *of*. Does a thought become a thought of X by being *like* X? Or is there some other relationship? No relationship will serve the purpose. For we can have thoughts of what does not exist – as in the case of my thought of a phoenix – and there is nothing, in such a case, for my thought to be related to. Moreover, even if we agree on the nature of the relationship – say, resemblance – and concentrate on the cases where there are things to be related to – say horses – there is still the problem of what *has* the relationship. A statue of a horse is a piece of stone or bronze resembling, with greater or less success, a real horse; but in the mind there is nothing corresponding to the stone or the bronze to bear the resemblance.

Aquinas's answer to the question 'What makes my thought of a horse a thought *of a horse?*' is that it is the very same thing as makes a real horse a horse: namely the form of horse. The form exists, individualised and materialised, in the real horse; it exists, universal and immaterial, in my mind; in the one case it has *esse naturale*, existence in nature; in the other case *esse intentionale*, existence in the mind. For a form, F-ness, to be, we said earlier, was for something or other to be F. We must now modify this and say, for a form F-ness to be, is either for something to be F or for somebody to be thinking of an F.

This doctrine must not be taken in any mystical sense. A modern admirer of Aquinas, Herbert McCabe, has well said:

The doctrine will be totally misunderstood if it is not recognised that it is intended to be *obvious*. It is not a description of a process by which we understand, if there is any such process. It is a platitude; it says 'What I have in mind when I know the nature of a cow is the nature of a cow and nothing else.' Now in case someone says 'But if the nature you have in your mind is that of a cow, surely your mind must be a cow – for to have the nature of an X simply means to be an X' St Thomas merely replies that to understand the nature of a cow is to have this nature precisely without being a cow, and this is what is made clear by saying that one has the nature in mind. To have it in mind doesn't mean anything except that you have the nature without being the thing whose nature it is. And this he calls 'having the nature intentionally'. The mind, for St Thomas, just is the locus of intentional being.

If the doctrine of intentional existence makes easy the question 'What makes a thought a thought of X?', it makes more striking the question 'What makes a thought A's thought?' There is nothing in the content of a thought that makes it one person's thought rather than another. Innumerable people beside myself believe that two and two make four: when I believe this, what makes the belief *my* belief? Aquinas insisted, against the Averroists, that such a thought is my thought and not the thought of any world-soul or supra-individual agent intellect. But to the question that *makes* them my thoughts his only answer is to point to the connection between the intellectual content of the thought and the mental images in which it is embodied. It is because these mental images are the products of my body that the intellectual thought is my thought. For many reasons, which it would take us too far to develop, this answer seems unsatisfactory. But as Wittgenstein once observed, it is not the answers which Aquinas gives, but the questions which he asks, which are the measure of his philosophical gifts.

Bibliographical note

Readers who want to know about St Thomas's life should read *Friar Thomas d'Aquino* by James Weisheipl O.P. (Blackwell, 1974). This is the most scholarly life in English, and my first chapter is very heavily dependent on it. G. K. Chesterton's *St Thomas Aquinas* (Hodder and Stoughton, 1933) is one of the most lively and popular books on St Thomas, but rarely gets close to the actual text of his writings: a more sober and philosophical treatment, which is not at all difficult to read, is Father Copleston's Pelican *Aquinas* (Penguin, 1955). A philosophically exciting, but highly controversial, account of Aquinas's metaphysics is the article by Peter Geach in *Three Philosophers*, by Anscombe and Geach (Blackwell, 1961). The best book in English about Aquinas's philosophy of mind is Bernard Lonergan's *Verbum: Word and Idea in Aquinas* (Notre Dame, 1967). It is densely packed with ideas and rewards the hard work of reading it. I have edited an anthology of articles on Aquinas by contemporary philosophers under the title *Aquinas: a collection of critical essays* (Macmillan, 1969).

The *Summa Theologiae* has recently been translated into English in sixty volumes in the Blackfriars edition (Eyre and Spottiswoode, 1963-75). The translations are of uneven value, but many are excellent, and all volumes contain useful information and the Latin text as well as the English. The *Summa contra Gentiles* has been translated by A. C. Pegis and others as *On the Truth of the Catholic Faith* (Random House, 1955).

Index